APR - - 2010

Pakistan

Other Books of Related Interest:

Opposing Viewpoints Series

India

Islam

The Middle East

Refugees

The World Trade Organization

At Issue Series

How Should the U.S. Proceed in Afghanistan?

What Role Should the U.S. Play in the Middle East?

Women in Islam

Current Controversies Series

Afghanistan

Fair Trade

Immigration

The World Economy

"Congress shall make no law . . . abridging the freedom of speech, or of the press."

First Amendment to the U.S. Constitution

The basic foundation of our democracy is the First Amendment guarantee of freedom of expression. The Opposing Viewpoints Series is dedicated to the concept of this basic freedom and the idea that it is more important to practice it than to enshrine it.

Pakistan

Laura Egendorf, Book Editor

GREENHAVEN PRESS
A part of Gale, Cengage Learning

Detroit • New York • San Francisco • New Haven, Conn • Waterville, Maine • London

Christine Nasso, *Publisher*
Elizabeth Des Chenes, *Managing Editor*

© 2010 Greenhaven Press, a part of Gale, Cengage Learning.

Articles in Greenhaven Press anthologies are often edited for length to meet page require-ments. In addition, original titles of these works are changed to clearly present the main thesis and to explicitly indicate the author's opinion. Every effort is made to ensure that Greenhaven Press accurately reflects the original intent of the authors. Every effort has been made to trace the owners of copyrighted material.

Cover photograph © Lichtmeister/Dreamstime.com.

LIBRARY OF CONGRESS CATALOGING-IN-PUBLICATION DATA

Egendorf, Laura K., 1973 / -Pakistan / Laura Egendorf.
    p. cm. -- (Opposing viewpoints)
    Includes bibliographical references and index.
    ISBN 978-0-7377-4538-2 (hardcover) -- ISBN 978-0-7377-4539-9 (pbk.)
    1. Pakistan--Politics and government--1988- 2. Pakistan--Economic conditions.
    3. Pakistan--Social conditions. 4. Pakistan--Foreign relations. 5. Security,
International--Pakistan. 6. National security--Pakistan. I. Title.
    DS389.E37 2010
    954.9105'3--dc22
                                                            2009044266

Printed in the United States of America
1 2 3 4 5 6 7 14 13 12 11 10

Contents

Chapter 3: What Should the U.S. Role Be in Pakistan?

Chapter 4: What Is the Future of Pakistan?

Why Consider Opposing Viewpoints?

> "The only way in which a human being can make some approach to knowing the whole of a subject is by hearing what can be said about it by persons of every variety of opinion and studying all modes in which it can be looked at by every character of mind. No wise man ever acquired his wisdom in any mode but this."
>
> *John Stuart Mill*

In our media-intensive culture it is not difficult to find differing opinions. Thousands of newspapers and magazines and dozens of radio and television talk shows resound with differing points of view. The difficulty lies in deciding which opinion to agree with and which "experts" seem the most credible. The more inundated we become with differing opinions and claims, the more essential it is to hone critical reading and thinking skills to evaluate these ideas. Opposing Viewpoints books address this problem directly by presenting stimulating debates that can be used to enhance and teach these skills. The varied opinions contained in each book examine many different aspects of a single issue. While examining these conveniently edited opposing views, readers can develop critical thinking skills such as the ability to compare and contrast authors' credibility, facts, argumentation styles, use of persuasive techniques, and other stylistic tools. In short, the Opposing Viewpoints Series is an ideal way to attain the higher-level thinking and reading skills so essential in a culture of diverse and contradictory opinions.

In addition to providing a tool for critical thinking, Opposing Viewpoints books challenge readers to question their own strongly held opinions and assumptions. Most people form their opinions on the basis of upbringing, peer pressure, and personal, cultural, or professional bias. By reading carefully balanced opposing views, readers must directly confront new ideas as well as the opinions of those with whom they disagree. This is not to simplistically argue that everyone who reads opposing views will—or should—change his or her opinion. Instead, the series enhances readers' understanding of their own views by encouraging confrontation with opposing ideas. Careful examination of others' views can lead to the readers' understanding of the logical inconsistencies in their own opinions, perspective on why they hold an opinion, and the consideration of the possibility that their opinion requires further evaluation.

Evaluating Other Opinions

To ensure that this type of examination occurs, Opposing Viewpoints books present all types of opinions. Prominent spokespeople on different sides of each issue as well as well-known professionals from many disciplines challenge the reader. An additional goal of the series is to provide a forum for other, less known, or even unpopular viewpoints. The opinion of an ordinary person who has had to make the decision to cut off life support from a terminally ill relative, for example, may be just as valuable and provide just as much insight as a medical ethicist's professional opinion. The editors have two additional purposes in including these less known views. One, the editors encourage readers to respect others' opinions—even when not enhanced by professional credibility. It is only by reading or listening to and objectively evaluating others' ideas that one can determine whether they are worthy of consideration. Two, the inclusion of such viewpoints encourages the important critical thinking skill of objectively evaluating an author's credentials and bias. This evaluation will illuminate an author's reasons for taking a particular stance on an issue and will aid in readers' evaluation of the author's ideas.

It is our hope that these books will give readers a deeper understanding of the issues debated and an appreciation of the complexity of even seemingly simple issues when good and honest people disagree. This awareness is particularly important in a democratic society such as ours in which people enter into public debate to determine the common good. Those with whom one disagrees should not be regarded as enemies but rather as people whose views deserve careful examination and may shed light on one's own.

Thomas Jefferson once said that "difference of opinion leads to inquiry, and inquiry to truth." Jefferson, a broadly educated man, argued that "if a nation expects to be ignorant and free . . . it expects what never was and never will be." As individuals and as a nation, it is imperative that we consider the opinions of others and examine them with skill and discernment. The Opposing Viewpoints Series is intended to help readers achieve this goal.

David L. Bender and Bruno Leone,
Founders

Introduction

> *"By re-igniting the Pakistani-Indian peace process and engaging Kashmiris in dialogue—along with Pakistanis and Indians—the United States can provide assistance in resolving the Kashmir problem."*
>
> —Ershad Mahmud,
> political analyst

> *"From the Indian perspective, there is a short answer to the question on what the Obama administration should do about Kashmir as part of its [Afghanistan-Pakistan] strategy: nothing."*
>
> —C. Raja Mohan,
> professor of international studies,
> Nanyang Technological University,
> Singapore

Pakistan's closest neighbor, India, is considered by much of its population to also be its greatest enemy, and much of the conflict between the two nations centers around one part of India, Kashmir. Pakistan believes that Kashmir ought to be under its control, a charge that India disputes. Solutions have been sought to end the impasse, but the problem has persisted for more than half a century. One possible solution is U.S. involvement, but the role the United States should play has been disputed.

The conflict began after India and Pakistan were partitioned into two separate nations in 1947. At that time, Kashmir had the choice as to which country it wanted to join, and its then-king opted for India. However, Pakistan believes that

Kashmir was forced to become part of India and that its citizens were never given the choice to decide. In fact, India promised that a referendum would be held so that Kashmir's citizens could affirm the decision made by their ruler, but no such vote has ever been held. In the opinion of Jyoti Thottam, in an article for *Time International*, India continues to maintain its hold on Kashmir as a way to show that it is superior to Pakistan. Thottam writes, "To hold on to Kashmir, even by force, was to pledge, implicitly, that the people of Kashmir would be better off as a part of India than as a part of Pakistan."

Violence in Kashmir, caused in part by Kashmiri separatists that have fought to expel Indian troops from their region, has killed more than 80,000 people and displaced hundreds of thousands. A war between Pakistan and India over that land would be even deadlier, and potentially have worldwide implications because both nations possess nuclear weapons. Consequently, some people believe that the United States must help end the conflict. However, this is not a universally held view.

One suggestion is that the United States could serve as a mediator between the two nations. Political analyst Ershad Mahmud, in an article for *Common Ground News*, contends that the United States should send a special envoy to Kashmir who would promote dialogue between Pakistan and India. Mahmud's view is supported by Meghan O'Sullivan, who served as a deputy national security adviser in the George W. Bush administration. She argues that U.S. involvement is necessary because it will help solve Pakistan's internal problems. According to O'Sullivan, "Pakistan's ability to deal with Taliban and other extremists on its western border is hampered by its preoccupation with India, its traditional adversary to the east. India has resisted U.S. mediation on Kashmir in the past, but the growing U.S.-India strategic relationship may now make American involvement possible."

On the other hand, C. Raja Mohan, an Indian strategic analyst and professor of international studies, is among those who contend that the U.S. should not place itself in the middle of the conflict because India and Pakistan have made important progress with back-channel negotiations, and increased U.S. involvement would ignore the significance of such efforts. His view is supported by India's minister of state for external affairs, Anand Sharma. In a February 2009 interview, he declared, "There's no question of any outside mediation. It's bilateral. Even Pakistan agrees. We have agreements between the two countries, and we need to talk. But as far as Kashmir for us is concerned, even vis-a-vis Pakistan, Kashmir is an internal matter." As of the summer of 2009, the Indian point of view appears to be the one that has been adopted by the Barack Obama administration.

The dispute over Kashmir is just one of the many problems that Pakistan is facing. In *Opposing Viewpoints: Pakistan,* the authors look at the key issues surrounding Pakistan in the following chapters: What Are the Internal Problems Facing Pakistan? How Can Pakistan Address Terrorism? What Should the U.S. Role Be in Pakistan? and What Is the Future of Pakistan? Located as it is in the hotbed of much of the world's most serious political problems, the fate of Pakistan could impact people around the world.

CHAPTER 1

What Are the Internal Problems Facing Pakistan?

Chapter Preface

Fighting along the border between Pakistan and Afghanistan has created a situation where 300,000 Pakistani are now living in refugee camps. Life in these crowded camps means having little to eat and unsanitary living conditions. As would be expected, diseases run rampant in the camps. Health problems include diarrhea, malaria, scabies, and acute respiratory infection.

The health woes are even more acute for females, who are often unable to receive treatment because cultural mores often forbid male doctors from treating women, and there aren't enough female doctors. Female and male patients also suffer from a lack of funding for health care in the camps. According to the United Nations, $37 million is needed to meet the basic health needs of the refugees.

Pakistan is also one of only five nations where the poliovirus still exists. Although vaccinations would eradicate the disease, many families refuse because religious clerics have labeled the polio vaccine an American plot to sterilize Muslims. According to the *Pakistan Health Cluster Bulletin*, a publication of the World Health Organization, 5.4 million children under the age of five who live either in the camps or within the North West Frontier Province and Federally Administered Tribal Areas need vaccinations.

The health problems in the refugee camps and surrounding areas may not be an issue for all of Pakistan, but the country is facing a variety of internal problems that make for a challenging future. The contributors to this chapter evaluate several issues critical to Pakistani life.

> *"USAID increases access to education for Pakistanis by rehabilitating inadequate and damaged school facilities, and building new schools."*

Pakistan's Educational System Is Problematic

U.S. Agency for International Development (USAID)

In the following viewpoint, the U.S. Agency for International Development (USAID) communicates the poor quality of Pakistani schools and how it aims to improve them. According to the article, nearly half of the country's population cannot read and teacher performance and education quality need improvement. USAID is developing projects to improve and increase teacher qualifications and it is enlarging school-feeding programs in order to increase school attendance for Pakistani children. USAID is a United States government organization that seeks to help countries overseas who are struggling to make a better life.

As you read, consider the following questions:

1. According to the article, how many Pakistanis cannot read?

2. What is one way that USAID seeks to ensure more Pakistani children attend school?

"Partnership For Education," USAID.gov, August 5, 2009. Reproduced by permission.

3. According to the viewpoint, what program funded by USAID gives many Pakistani students the opportunity to obtain doctorates and master's degrees in the U.S.?

Nearly 50 million Pakistanis (half the country's adult population) cannot read. Only 60 percent of Pakistani children complete 10 years of school, and only 10 percent complete 12 years. Since 2002, USAID's education program has invested over $682 million to reform and revitalize Pakistan's education system.

Increasing Access to Education

USAID increases access to education for Pakistanis by rehabilitating inadequate and damaged school facilities, and building new schools. It is constructing and equipping science and computer laboratories for teachers' colleges in several cities. USAID will upgrade and rehabilitate thousands of schools nationwide. This effort will include parents and communities in school management and planning. The need of girls will receive special attention. Adding to these efforts, USAID will fund the construction of additional schools. To ensure that more Pakistani children attend school and graduate, USAID is expanding a school-feeding program in the most food-insecure areas of Pakistan.

Improving Education Quality

To improve teacher performance and skills development, USAID's projects are upgrading the qualifications of current teachers and developing a comprehensive program for pre-service teacher training. Working closely with the Ministry of Education, USAID is developing national standards for accreditation and improving coordination among teacher training institutions. Together with the Higher Education Commission (HEC), USAID is working to institutionalize pre-service teacher education reforms at universities and colleges. By sup-

Madrassas and Religious Extremism

One thing is clear, the growth of the Madrassas [religious schools] in Pakistan reflects the ascendance of religious extremism in the country. The sources of this extremism are complex, but at least four factors have played a significant role: (1) The extensive Saudi funding for exporting Salafi/Wahhabiism to the subcontinent and for keeping religious reactionaries at bay in seminaries set up in regions at a distance from the Kingdom; (2) Reliance on religious elements by the military high command and civilian autocrats (like Benazir Bhutto and Nawaz Sharif) to promote anti-democratic agendas; (3) Anti-Americanism generated initially by the pro-Israeli U.S. commitment and fuelled subsequently by the U.S. invasions of Afghanistan and Iraq; and (4) The organizational zeal of the Jamaat-i-Islam which enabled it for the time being to gather disparate religious groups under the umbrella of the Muttahida Majlis-i-Amal (MMA)—the coalition of religious parties that won the provincial elections in the NWP [North West Frontier Province] and Balochistan in October 2002.

Robert Looney, "Reforming Pakistan's Educational System,"
Journal of Social, Political and Economic Studies, *Fall 2003.*

porting the National Education Management Information System (NEMIS), USAID ensures that education data is valid and is used for planning and management at the school and district levels. In other programs, USAID addresses students' classroom learning needs through child-centered teaching methods, curriculum pacing guides, and improvements to teaching and learning in math, science, computers and English.

Providing Easier Access
to Higher Education

To develop a cadre of experts and leaders in the areas of agriculture, science and technology, social science and business, USAID invests heavily in Pakistan's higher education institutions, merit- and needs-based scholarships and international exchanges. The merit- and needs-based scholarship program in collaboration with the HEC provides thousands of needy students with scholarships for degree programs at Pakistani universities. Pakistan has the largest Fulbright program in the world, which is funded by USAID, giving hundreds of Pakistani students the opportunities to obtain master's degrees and doctorates in the United States. USAID works with the HEC to develop a National Student Financial Aid System, which will ensure access to sources of funding including grants, work study and loans for students.

Assisting higher education institutions to better educate students, USAID supports university partnership programs between U.S. and two Pakistani universities, and also supports a college in Lahore in developing a four-year bachelor's degree program. USAID is assisting the Peshawar University's human rights faculty to build its capacity in legal education, human rights and gender.

Together with the Ministry of Science and Technology and HEC, USAID supports the Pakistan-U.S. Science and Technology Cooperative Program, implemented by the U.S. National Academy of Sciences, by providing grants to support collaboration between Pakistani and U.S. scientists, engineers and health care specialists. This will promote Pakistani expertise and development in agriculture, water, health, and environmental sciences.

> *"There is little or no evidence that madrassas produce terrorists capable of attacking the West."*

Pakistan's Educational System Does Not Foster Terrorism

Peter Bergen and Swati Pandey

The Muslim religious schools called madrassas do not breed terrorists, Peter Bergen and Swati Pandey maintain in the following viewpoint. The authors assert that while madrassas are common in Pakistan, investigations of terrorist attacks find that most terrorists did not attend that type of school. Furthermore, they note, most Pakistani children do not go to madrassas. The authors conclude that the United States should not view madrassas as a threat. Bergen is the author of Holy War, Inc. *and a fellow at the New America Foundation. Pandey is a research associate at the foundation, which is a public policy institute that seeks to find answers to the domestic and international problems facing the United States.*

Peter Bergen and Swati Pandey, "The Madrassas Myth: Muslim Religious Schools' Influence on Terrorism," *Washington Report on Middle East Affairs*, vol. 24, August 2005.

As you read, consider the following questions:

1. What percentage of the terrorists behind major attacks against the West had college degrees, as stated by the authors?

2. According to a World Bank-financed study cited by Bergen and Pandey, what percentage of Pakistani students attends madrassas?

3. In the view of the authors, how should we treat the money the U.S. spends on education and literacy in the Middle East and South Asia?

It is one of the widespread assumptions of the war on terrorism that the Muslim religious schools known as madrassas, catering to families that are often poor, are graduating students who become terrorists. Last year [2004,] Secretary of State Colin L. Powell denounced madrassas in Pakistan and several other countries as breeding grounds for "fundamentalists and terrorists." A year earlier, Secretary of Defense Donald H. Rumsfeld had queried in a leaked memorandum, "Are we capturing, killing or deterring and dissuading more terrorists every day than the madrassas and the radical clerics are recruiting, training and deploying against us?"

While madrassas may breed fundamentalists who have learned to recite the Qur'an in Arabic by rote, such schools do not teach the technical or linguistic skills necessary to be an effective terrorist. Indeed, there is little or no evidence that madrassas produce terrorists capable of attacking the West. And as a matter of national security, the United States doesn't need to worry about Muslim fundamentalists with whom we may disagree, but about terrorists who want to attack us.

More than Half of Terrorists Are College Educated

We examined the educational backgrounds of 75 terrorists behind some of the most significant recent terrorist attacks against Westerners. We found that a majority of them are college-educated, often in technical subjects like engineering. In the four attacks for which the most complete information about the perpetrators' educational levels is available—the World Trade Center bombing in 1993, the attacks on the American embassies in Kenya and Tanzania in 1998, the 9/11 [2001] attacks, and the Bali bombings in 2002—53 percent of the territories had either attended college or had received a college degree. As a point of reference, only 52 percent of Americans have been to college. The terrorists in our study thus appear, on average, to be as well educated as many Americans.

The 1993 World Trade Center attack involved 12 men, all of whom had a college education. The 9/11 pilots, as well as the secondary planners identified by the 9/11 commission, all attended Western universities, a prestigious and elite endeavor for anyone from the Middle East. Indeed, the lead 9/11 pilot, Mohamed Atta, had a degree from a German university in, of all things, urban preservation, while the operational planner of 9/11, Khalid Sheikh Mohammed, studied engineering in North Carolina. We also found that two-thirds of the 25 hijackers and planners involved in 9/11 had attended college.

Of the 75 terrorists we investigated, only nine had attended madrassas, and all of those played a role in one attack—the Bali bombing. Even in this instance, however, five college-educated "masterminds"—including two university lecturers—helped to shape the Bali plot.

Like the view that poverty drives terrorism—a notion that countless studies have debunked—the idea that madrassas are incubating the next generation of terrorists offers the soothing illusion that desperate, ignorant automatons [robot-like, non-thinking people] are attacking us rather than college graduates, as is often the case. In fact, two of the terrorists in our study had doctorates from Western universities, and two others were working toward their Ph.D.

Madrassas Education Is Not Useful for Terrorism

There is no evidence that any of the terrorists involved in major international terror attacks during the last four years ever enrolled as regular students in a madrasa [religious school], though they may have passed through madrasas on the way to terrorist training camps.

Given their total lack of Western education, madrasa students are not particularly useful to any modern day employer, including terrorist groups. They cannot blend into a Western nation or mount sophisticated operations requiring technical expertise. They lack linguistic ability and competence in even basic forms of technology because such skills are not generally taught at madrasas. Some madrasa students do not even have basic mathematical skills, necessary for mounting even moderately sophisticated terrorist operations.

C. Christine Fair and Husain Haqqani,
www.foreignpolicy.com, January 2006.

Madrassas Are Not Widely Attended in Pakistan

A World Bank-financed study that was published in April [2005] raises further doubts about the influence of madrassas in Pakistan, the country where the schools were thought to be the most influential and the most virulently anti-American. Contrary to the numbers cited in the report of the 9/11 commission, and to a blizzard of newspaper reports that 10 percent of Pakistani students study in madrassas, the study's authors found that fewer than 1 percent do so. If correct, this estimate would suggest that there are far more American children being home-schooled than Pakistani boys attending madrassas.

While madrassas are an important issue in education and development in the Muslim world, they are not and should not be considered a threat to the United States. The tens of millions of dollars spent every year by the United States through the State Department, the Middle East Partnership Initiative, and the Agency for International Development to improve education and literacy in the Middle East and South Asia should be applauded as the development aid it is and not as the counterterrorism effort it cannot be.

| *"Widespread economic distress will lead to increased public demonstrations, strikes and turmoil."*

Pakistan Has a Weak Economy

Sumit Ganguly

In the following viewpoint, Sumit Ganguly asserts that Pakistan's seemingly strong economy has unraveled. Ganguly argues that Pakistan is struggling economically because it relied too much on foreign dollars, with the government ignoring underlying issues such as low tax receipts and poor infrastructure. Ganguly concludes that Pakistan's leaders cannot ignore these problems because doing so could lead to an Islamist resurgence. Ganguly is the director of research at the Center on American and Global Security at Indiana University.

As you read, consider the following questions:

1. What is the poverty rate in Pakistan, as stated by Ganguly?

2. According to the author, where is Pakistan ranked in the United Nations' *Human Development Report*?

3. As explained by Ganguly, what made imports to Pakistan more expensive?

For much of his tenure, Pakistan's President, Gen. Pervez Musharraf, had two claims to fame: that he'd put the country on the path to moderation by marginalizing its Islamic radicals, and that his economic policies had helped spark dramatic economic growth (about 7 percent a year). Now the resurgence of the Taliban and its allies and a spate of suicide bombings have called the first claim into question. And while the recent accidental killing of Pakistani troops on the Afghan border, allegedly by coalition troops, have focused all attention on security matters, Musharraf's second supposed achievement is also unraveling: according to some Pakistani economists, the poverty rate recently hit 34 percent (up from 32 percent in 1999); the World Bank is now predicting a paltry 3.5 percent growth rate for the coming year, and the rupee is plummeting against the dollar.

Pakistan's Economy Depends on Foreign Dollars

What happened? The answer has less to do with Musharraf's declining power—he's now fighting for survival—than you might think. The country's economic boom never actually had much to do with the general's policies . . . Pakistan has always depended on the kindness of strangers. In the wake of 9/11 [2001], renewed ties with Washington brought substantial aid. Even before the $10 billion in U.S. military and economic assistance started to flow in, Pakistan's Western allies wrote off billions of dollars of debt, which helped bring the economy back to life. About the same time, many expatriates who'd parked their wealth in foreign banks began investing in their homeland's stock market. Their new strategy wasn't irrational; after the attacks on the United States, many Muslims in the West, regardless of their political or ideological proclivities, started coming under considerable government scrutiny. Suddenly investing back home became much more attractive.

The new aid, investments and remittances significantly buoyed Pakistan's economy. Yet Musharraf's military regime never used the opportunity to address the country's endemic underlying problems. Tax receipts remained low due to the government's reluctance to crack down on powerful business players, investment in infrastructure lagged, agricultural productivity stagnated and social services were neglected. Adult literacy is still only about 49 percent, and the [United Nations Development Progamme's] *Human Development Report* ranks Pakistan 136 out of 177 countries. Foreign investors, who'd been flooding the country's booming service sector to cater to its growing ranks of nouveau riche [newly rich], took note of these persistent flaws, and even the emergence of a democratically elected government in the February 2008 elections did little to allay their concerns. The worsening security situation—tragically underscored by the assassination of former prime minister Benazir Bhutto in December 2007—made the country's future seem all the more uncertain.

Foreign dollars thus soon started to dry up, and the underlying weakness of Pakistan's economy left it acutely vulnerable to other external shocks. When oil prices began to climb this spring, the country reeled, and as Pakistan's treasury faced a dramatic outflow of funds (Pakistan buys most of its oil abroad and has to pay in hard currency), confidence in the rupee fell precipitously. This, in turn, made imports more expensive. The rise in global food prices also hit ordinary Pakistanis hard and, as they cut back on consumption, sent the already shaky economy into a tailspin.

Economic Problems Could Lead to the Rise of Islamists

All this bodes ill for the country's immediate future. The new coalition government has already deadlocked, mired in an unseemly squabble over the reinstatement of a number of Supreme Court judges arbitrarily dismissed by Musharraf.

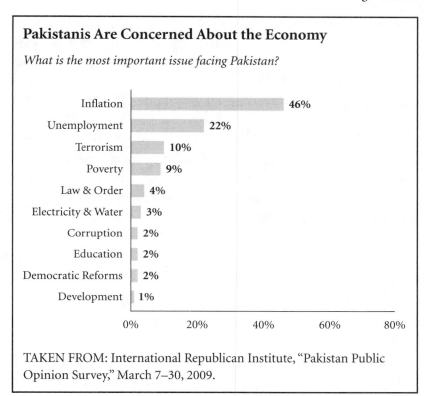

Pakistanis Are Concerned About the Economy

What is the most important issue facing Pakistan?

Issue	Percent
Inflation	46%
Unemployment	22%
Terrorism	10%
Poverty	9%
Law & Order	4%
Electricity & Water	3%
Corruption	2%
Education	2%
Democratic Reforms	2%
Development	1%

TAKEN FROM: International Republican Institute, "Pakistan Public Opinion Survey," March 7–30, 2009.

(Nawaz Sharif, a former prime minister and leader of one half of the coalition, wants to reinstate them; Asif Zardari, Bhutto's widower and the head of the other faction, doesn't.) All these leaders are far too preoccupied with their own survival at the moment to deal with Pakistan's pressing economic ills. Yet this inattention could prove critical, for economic drift will only exacerbate the country's political woes. Widespread economic distress will lead to increased public demonstrations, strikes and turmoil. Under these conditions, Islamist forces could easily win broad support by promising facile [easy] remedies, such as the imposition of Sharia [Islamic law] and an end to military cooperation with the United States.

An Islamist resurgence would put the country's military, which has recently been accused of starting to appease radicals in the border regions, in an awkward spot, forcing it to decide between trying to co-opt the Islamists and crack down. An Islamist surge could also damage Pakistan's fragile relationship with India, which both countries have tried to repair in recent years. From a U.S. standpoint, all this would be a disaster, since an economically anemic and politically unstable Pakistan wouldn't be able to offer much help against Al Qaeda and the Taliban. Islamabad [Pakistan's capital] can still switch course if it ends the factional squabbling in the government, restores the independence of the judiciary, professionalizes the police and paramilitary forces and keeps the military in check. But time is fast running out.

| "[Pakistan's] growth is broadly based
and is evenly distributed across sectors
of the economy."

Pakistan Has
a Strong Economy

Economic Review

In the following viewpoint, Economic Review *contends that Pakistan has a strong and growing economy. According to the magazine, Pakistan's economic growth is based on foreign investment, macroeconomic policies, and growth in the services sector. In addition, the magazine notes, the country has benefited from the expansion of the global economy.* Economic Review *is a publication of the Federal Reserve Bank of Atlanta.*

As you read, consider the following questions:

1. According to *Economic Review,* how much did Pakistan's economy grow in fiscal year 2006–2007?

2. Why has construction performed strongly, as explained by the magazine?

3. By how much did the global economy expand in 2005–2006, according to *Economic Review*?

"Growth and Investment," *Economic Review,* February/March 2008, pp. 6–7. Reproduced by permission.

Pakistan's economy continues to maintain its strong growth momentum for the fifth year in a row in the fiscal year 2006–07. With economic growth at 7.0 percent in the current fiscal year, Pakistan's economy has grown at an average rate of almost 7.0 percent per annum during the last five years. This brisk pace of expansion on sustained basis has enabled Pakistan to position itself as one of the fastest growing economies of the Asian region. The growth that the economy has sustained for the last five years is underpinned by dynamism in industry, agriculture and services, and the emergence of a new investment cycle supported by strong growth in domestic demand. The State Bank of Pakistan (SBP) attempted to shave off some of the excess demand which was causing general price hike by changing its monetary policy stance to aggressive tightening. Successive hikes in policy rates have led to higher interest rates across the spectrum, but higher inflation means that real interest rates remain low and their dampening effect on growth remained minimal. The prerequisites for a sustained economic growth appear to have gained firm footing during the last five years.

Investment in Pakistan Has Increased

The past few years of strong economic growth has brought Pakistan to the attention of an ever-wider set of investors and leading companies of the world. Resultantly, foreign investment has attained new heights and likely to touch $6.5 billion mark this year [2008]. Never before have conditions been so well aligned for a major push toward sustainable growth and poverty reduction.

The current economic upturn is substantially different from the occasional economic rebounds of short duration that Pakistan has witnessed in the recent past. The gradual build-up of the investment momentum this time also suggests that investment recovery is likely to be more sustainable. The monetary tightening has therefore not derailed the ongoing

Unemployment Is Declining in Pakistan

Sharp rise in inflation worldwide during 2004–06 and concurrent inflationary pressures triggered Pakistan's then stable inflation to rise to 7.8 percent at end 2007. Unemployment in Pakistan was continually declining since 2003. The Government's effective macroeconomic policies contained unemployment at its lowest level in the region. Strong employment generation, particularly, in the services sector and textile industry facilitated a decline in unemployment. Increases in socially-oriented spending and high workers' remittances resulted in the rise in job satisfaction. As the outcome of these measures, unemployment declined from 7.7 percent in 2004 to 6.2 percent in 2006.

Economic Cooperation Organization,
Country Report: Pakistan, 2008, www.ecosecretariat.org.

economic upsurge because balance between sustaining the growth momentum and containing inflation is maintained.

Many Sectors Have Seen Growth

Real GDP [gross domestic product] grew strongly at 7.0 percent in 2006–07 as against the revised estimates of 6.6 percent for last year and 7.0 percent growth target for the year. When viewed at the backdrop of rising and volatile energy prices and fallout of the earthquake of October 8, 2005, Pakistan's growth performance for the year has been impressive. The growth is broadly based and is evenly distributed across sectors of the economy. Services sector, though witnessed slight deceleration in growth, still has spearheaded the movement towards higher growth trajectory. The services sector continued to perform strongly and grew by 8.0 percent as against the target of 7.0 percent and last year's actual growth of 9.6 percent. Large-scale manufacturing grew by 8.8 percent as against 10.7 percent of last year and 12.5 percent target for the year, exhibiting signs of moderation on account of higher capacity utilization on the one hand and stabilization of demand for industrial products especially consumer durables on the other. Agriculture sector bounced back from lacklustre performance of last year and particularly its major crop sector recovered strongly from a negative growth of 4.1 percent to a positive growth of 7.6 percent. Livestock, a major component of agriculture, exhibited signs of moderation from its buoyant growth of 7.5 percent last year to 4.3 percent in 2006–07. Construction too continued its strong showing, partly helped by activity in private housing market, spending on physical infrastructure, and reconstruction activities in earthquake affected areas private consumption rising by 4.1 percent and investment spending maintaining its strong momentum at 20.6 percent increase in real investment. While strong economic growth is underpinned by the sound macroeconomic policies pursued by the government, Pakistan has also benefited from the buoyant global economic environment undeterred by the rising and volatile energy prices. The global economy continued its strong expansion. The expansion is becoming geographically more broad-based, and global growth is expected to remain strong over the near term. Inflation and inflationary expectations remained tamed but there are downside risks, including those related to continued high and volatile oil prices, abrupt tightening of global financial conditions, and a rise in protectionist tendencies.

Domestic macroeconomic reforms teamed with an expanding world economy have helped in sustaining prolonged period of macroeconomic stability. In 2004–05, global growth at 5.3 percent was the strongest in thirty years. Growth in 2005–06 moderated to 4.9 percent and then expected to accelerate to 5.4 percent in 2006–07. The remarkable expansion seen in the past couple of years has been broad-based with almost every region of the world experiencing buoyant growth—including South Asia.

"*Pakistan has become increasingly important in the jihadist strategy since Al Qaeda was driven out of Afghanistan.*"

Pakistan Is a Front for Al Qaeda

Ed Blanche

In the following viewpoint, Ed Blanche asserts that the terrorist network Al Qaeda is becoming a growing problem in Pakistan. However, argues Blanche, the Pakistani government has shown a reluctance to crack down on Islamic militancy. Instead, he contends, Pakistan's army has focused its attention on India. Should Al Qaeda gain power in Pakistan, it would cause instability not only there but in Afghanistan as well. Blanche is a journalist who specializes in Middle East issues.

As you read, consider the following questions:

1. In the author's view, what will happen if the U.S. government props up President Musharraf?

2. According to Nigel Inkster, as cited by Blanche, which "neo-Taliban" group is the biggest threat to Pakistan and other nations?

Ed Blanche, "Pakistan: A Major Stepping Stone in Al Qaeda's Global Strategy," *The Middle East*, April 2008. Copyright © 2008 IC Publications Ltd. Reproduced by permission.

3. Why was the assassination of Benazir Bhutto of particular concern to Israel, as explained by the author?

Pakistan is now the main frontline in Al Qaeda's war and if that country goes under, the Middle East will suffer.

Pakistan is a vital bastion of the US presence in the Middle East and the Americans would find it extremely difficult, if not impossible, to hold their ground in Afghanistan and in the Gulf if the jihadists [those espousing "holy war"] gained even a measure of power in Islamabad [Pakistan's capital].

Pakistan Is in Political Disarray

With the assassination of former prime minister Benazir Bhutto, in a suicide bombing on 27 December [2007], and the wave of violence that has since engulfed the country, the Americans fear radical Islamists now threaten the very survival of Pakistan as a state.

President [Pervez] Musharraf's Pakistan Muslim League-Quad-e-Azam party fared badly in parliamentary elections held on 18 February [2008]. Bhutto's Pakistan People's Party and the Pakistan Muslim League (Nawaz), led by former Prime Nawaz Sharif, scored heavily. But the elections appeared to throw Pakistan into ever deeper disarray.

Although the two moderate opposition parties talked of forming a coalition, they have a long history of enmity. They wooed Islamist politicians, but seem to have little in common with them beyond booting Musharraf out of power.

And, to Washington's dismay, they have shown a marked reluctance in the past to crack down on Islamist militants. Musharraf's military-backed rule is clearly at an end, and if the US seeks to prop him up it will fuel the political turmoil by intensifying anti-American anger that is already widespread.

On the face of it, Pakistan remains incapable of countering the mounting threat from "Pashtunistan," the bandlands on both sides of the Afghan-Pakistani border where the resurgent Taliban, Al Qaeda and their allies have built up a formidable power base.

Too Slow to Respond to the Threat

The prospect of a nuclear-armed Pakistan in the hands of Islamist militants is a nightmare for the Americans and their allies, particularly Israel. Islamabad insists its nuclear arsenal is secure, but doubts persist.

The director of US intelligence, retired admiral Mike McConnell, delivered an unusually strong warning about the upsurge of violence in Pakistan to the US Senate Select Committee on Intelligence on 6 February [2008]. "In the last year," he said, "the number of terrorist attacks and deaths were greater than the past six years combined. What's happened is that Pakistan has now recognised that this is an existential threat to its very survival."

This awareness of the gravity of the crisis has prompted Pakistani leaders to "be more aggressive in getting control of the situation" by cracking down on Al Qaeda and the Taliban who for years have been nurtured by groups of officials in the Pakistani military and intelligence services, in particular the Inter-Services Intelligence department.

But Musharraf's move was too late. The army, now commanded by Musharraf's annointed successor, General Ashfaq Kayani, kept out of the electoral process for the first time in many years, but it is likely to maintain its overwhelming influence in political affairs.

An early test of Kayani's intentions will be whether he will move against the considerable number of Islamist sympathisers within the military and intelligence establishment, who nurtured the Taliban in the first place as a buffer against India and who continue to help the militants.

A Struggle to Stabilize the Middle East

The US alliance with Musharraf began after 9/11 [2001] and has enabled the Americans to protect the southern flank of the oil-rich Gulf. As one British commentator observed: "It would be a disaster if the US lost a position of influence with the Arab oil-producing countries. Trouble in Pakistan means trouble in the oil market. If the political situation in the Middle East were to get worse, the oil price would go higher and the global shortage of funds would become more serious."

The strategic implications of the crisis in Pakistan, and its impact in neighbouring Afghanistan, extend throughout the Middle East, and deepen the inability of the US, already badly stretched in Iraq, to stabilise the region it plunged into upheaval when it invaded Iraq in March 2003.

The danger facing Pakistan "combined with the continuing threat of Turkish incursions into Iraqi Kurdistan and another war between US-backed Ethiopia and Eritrea have added to the growing impression that Washington has ever more become hostage to forces and personalities far beyond its control or understanding," according to Washington-based commentator Jim Lobe.

"Worse, if events turn out badly, these crises could deal devastating setbacks to Washington's hopes of bolstering 'moderate' forces against its perceived enemies, be they Sunni jihadis or the allegedly Tehran-led 'axis' of Syria, Hizbullah and Hamas."

The demise of Musharraf's army-backed regime has been compared in some quarters to the loss of Iran in 1979 when the shah [hereditary monarch, or king], like Musharraf a staunch US ally, was overthrown and Ayatollah Ruhollah Khomeini took over. Some analysts say that the violent upheaval in Pakistan mirrors the Islamic revolution in Iran—but with a big difference. Pakistan is a nuclear power.

Gary Sick, an Iran expert and Columbia professor who guided US policy on Iran during the [President Jimmy] Carter years, says the US bet everything on Musharraf in the war against terror, just as it did with the shah as a bulwark against Soviet expansion. "We've bet the farm on one man, in this case Pervez Musharraf, and we have no fallback position, no alternative strategy in the event that it does not work," said Sick.

The Pakistani Army Must Keep Control

According to one Pakistani analyst, the perceptive and well-connected Syed Saleem Shahzad, the aim of the jihadis behind the mushrooming insurgency is to extend it from its epicentre in the wild tribal belt along the border with Afghanistan "into a large-scale offensive to bring down the central government, or force the government to support their cause."

Some analysts doubt that the jihadists will take over the state. Kamran Bokhari of the Texas-based security consultancy Strategic Forecasting, noted: "Though there are many, many reasons for concern in Pakistan, state breakdown is not one of them. Such an extreme outcome would require the fracturing of the military and/or the army's loss of control over the country—neither of which is about to happen . . ."

"Pakistan's army is a highly disciplined organisation . . . The generals know their personal wellbeing is only as good as their collective ability to function as a unified and disciplined force—one that can guarantee the security of the state," he said. "It is extremely unlikely that jihadism—despite the presence of jihadist sympathisers within the junior and mid-level ranks—will cause fissures within the army."

But the army, despite massive US aid since 9/11, has shown neither the will nor the capability to crash the unrest in the tribal zones, or to prevent it spreading into Pakistan's major cities. The military has been structured to fight wars with Pakistan's arch-rival India, not conduct a major counter-insurgency campaign. One Western officer said the Pakistani army was "a dinosaur of an institution."

Heavy losses in the fighting in the northwest has affected the army's morale. On top of that, the majority Punjabis dominate the military while the insurgents are made up almost exclusively of rival Pashtuns, so there is a serious risk of Pakistan fracturing along ethnic lines that Osama bin Laden could exploit.

Jane's Terrorism and Security Monitor, an authoritative London-based newsletter, concludes that even under a new elected government "mainstream politics will continue to be characterised by the vicious struggles, conspiracy theories and unconstitutional antics that benefit the extremists on the fringes of society . . ."

"The tribal areas will continue to provide Afghan, Arab, Central Asian and western jihadists with sanctuary and training grounds, ensuring Pakistan remains a preeminent international security concern for the foreseeable future. While the militants are too weak to take over the nuclear-bomb armed country, as some fear, they are clearly capable of destabilising it. Pakistan's future remains hard to predict, but it will certainly be violent."

Pakistan Has Become a Center of Terrorism

Pakistan has become increasingly important in the jihadist strategy since Al Qaeda was driven out of Afghanistan by US-led forces in late 2001—although President George W. Bush failed to grasp that. He has long insisted that Iraq is the key battleground in the war against global terrorism.

But according to US military sources, intercepted Al Qaeda communications have indicated that Al Qaeda Central saw Iraq primarily as a giant trap in which to keep the US military pinned down while the jihadis rebuilt their strength in Waziristan and moved towards their strategic objectives.

Pakistani Intelligence Has Helped Al Qaeda

Pakistani government support for the Taliban officially ended after 9/11 [2001], when Pervez Musharraf, an army general who had seized power in a 1999 coup, pledged to assist the U.S. war on terrorism. But not everyone was on board. Some in Pakistan's InterServices Intelligence spy agency (ISI) played a double game, turning a blind eye when members of the Taliban leadership and al-Qaeda escaped to Pakistan's Federally Administered Tribal Areas (FATA) along the border with Afghanistan. FATA's un-governed spaces provided the ideal sanctuary for militant groups on the run. Musharraf made a halfhearted at-tempt, at Washington's behest, to stop the Afghan Taliban and al-Qaeda from waging insurgency across the border. But that only inflamed tensions; the Afghan militants turned their rage on his government, winning to their cause local Pakistanis with whom they have close ties.

Aryn Baker, "The Central Front,"
Time, September 11, 2008.

Recent events in the United Kingdom [UK] and Europe indicate that terrorist groups are being run directly from Paki-stan these days. Admiral Michael Mullen, chairman of the US Joint Chiefs of Staff, warned in testimony to the Senate in early February that the next attack on the US would likely be launched by jihadi cells controlled from that region.

The International Institute for Strategic Affairs in London warned in February that "neo-Taliban" groups operating in Pakistan's tribal belt are becoming a global menace. Nigel Ink-ster, who heads the institute's risk analysis unit, said: "They have the potential to turn a local threat into a transnational threat. There is some evidence they were involved with the assassination of Benazir Bhutto and that they have dispatched terrorists to the UK and Spain."

Inkster, a former director of operations for Britain's Secret Intelligence Service, popularly known as MI6, said one group in particular was probably the fastest growing threat—Tehrik-e Taliban, the Pakistani wing of the Taliban and a loose alliance of some 40 jihadist organisations and tribal groups in the northwestern war zone.

It is led by Baitullah Mehsud, a Pashtun warlord who the Musharraf government accused of masterminding the Bhutto assassination. He has denied that charge but the CIA [U.S. Central Intelligence Agency] backs Islamabad in pointing the finger at him. Mehsud has built up his power since 9/11 by aiding Al Qaeda and the Taliban after they were driven from Afghanistan in late 2001.

Inkster said Tehrik-e Taliban has "very recently shown an inclination to link themselves to a wider agenda. Because of the wider ramifications of unrest in the region, the Pakistani neo-Taliban, as it is called, has become a potent and growing threat. Mehsud has linked himself formally with the Afghan Taliban and has been quoted about the need to combat the United States and Britain, so he's adopting a wider political agenda."

The unprecedented jihadist insurgency is rooted in the northwestern tribal lands along the mountainous border with Afghanistan where the unruly ultra-conservative Pashtuns have traditionally shunned the central government. But this militancy, which has given new life to Al Qaeda and the Taliban, has widened since Benazir Bhutto was assassinated.

The country has been ravaged by a series of suicide bombings, unheard of in Pakistan until a couple of years ago. These have largely been directed against the military and security establishment, but hundreds of civilians have perished as the bloodletting has for the first time spread to the major urban areas such as Islamabad, the capital, and Karachi, the country's commercial hub.

Understanding Al Qaeda's Objectives

The emergence of Al Qaeda's new strength in Pakistan's tribal belt, which is sometimes termed "the virulent core of a growing insurgency," is largely comprised of a new generation of radicalised militants, ideologically linked to Osama bin Laden's movement and with little loyalty to their local religious or tribal leaders.

For many in Israel, Bhutto's assassination removed another barrier shielding the Jewish state from the Islamic bomb. Bhutto was reported to have been reaching out to Israel before her ill-fated return to Pakistan, as indeed has Musharraf himself.

If Al Qaeda and its fellow travellers succeed in undermining the Musharraf regime, or even winning a small share in power with other Islamists, Arab regimes allied with the US should also beware because for bin Laden they are classed as the 'near enemy'.

This is a particular objective of Ayman Al Zawahiri, ostensibly Al Qaeda's No. 2 but increasingly seen as responsible for driving strategy and operational planning within the jihadist network. Both bin Laden and Zawahiri are believed to operate from sanctuaries in Waziristan.

In Afghanistan, the Taliban, aided by Al Qaeda, has steadily intensified its war against the US-backed government of President Hamid Karzai over the last two years. US and NATO [North Atlantic Treaty Organization] officials say the violence has reached its highest levels since the US-led invasion against the Taliban and its allies in 2001.

Afghanistan faces even more upheaval if Pakistan faces further unrest. "Pakistan is the first stepping stone in Al Qaeda's global strategy," says Pakistani commentator Syed Saleem Shahzad.

> "*Many across the spectrum of Pakistani society express anger at U.S. global foreign policy.*"

Anti-American Views Are a Problem in Pakistan

K. Alan Kronstadt

K. Alan Kronstadt asserts in the following viewpoint that Pakistan is one of the world's most anti-American nations. He contends that Pakistanis distrust the United States and believe that America wants to weaken the Muslim world. According to Kronstadt, one possible reason for these views is that some of the Muslim religious schools, called madrassas, are known to teach extremism. Kronstadt is a specialist in South Asian affairs for the Congressional Research Service.

As you read, consider the following questions:

1. According to a June 2006 poll cited by the author, what percentage of Pakistanis held a favorable opinion of the United States?

2. How many madrassas are in Pakistan, as stated by Kronstadt?

K. Alan Kronstadt, *CRS Report for Congress: Pakistan-U.S. Relations*, pp. 73–77.

3. According to the author, how much money has the United States allocated for education aid to Pakistan since 2002?

With some 160 million citizens, Pakistan is the world's second-most populous Muslim country, and the nation's very foundation grew from a perceived need to create a homeland for South Asian Muslims in the wake of decolonization. However, religious-based political parties traditionally have fared poorly in national elections. An unexpected outcome of the country's 2002 polls saw the Muttahida Majlis-e-Amal (MMA or United Action Front), a coalition of six Islamic parties, win 11% of the popular vote. It also gained control of the provincial assembly in the North West Frontier Province (NWFP) and led a coalition in the Baluchistan assembly. These Pashtun-majority western provinces border Afghanistan, where U.S.-led counterterrorism operations are ongoing. In 2003, the NWFP provincial assembly passed a Shariat (Islamic law) bill. In both 2005 and 2006, the same assembly passed a Hasba (accountability) bill that many fear could create a parallel Islamic legal body. Pakistan's Supreme Court, responding to petitions by President [Pervez] Musharraf's government, rejected most of this legislation as unconstitutional, but in 2007 it upheld most of a modified Hasba bill resubmitted by the NWFP assembly. Such developments alarm Pakistan's moderates and Musharraf himself has decried any attempts to "Talibanize" regions of Pakistan. The Islamist coalition was ousted from power in Peshawar and suffered major electoral losses nationwide when February 2008 polls saw the secular Pashtun nationalist Awami National Party take over the NWFP government.

Anti-American Views Are Prevalent in Pakistan

Pakistan's Islamists are notable for expressions of anti-American sentiment, at times calling for "jihad" [holy war]

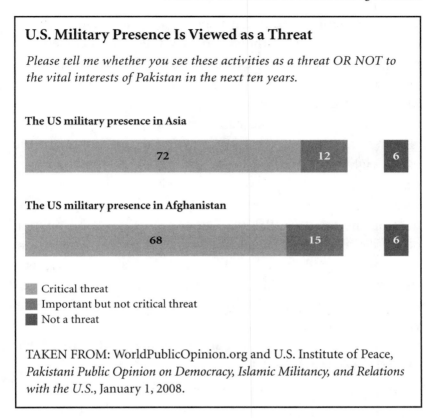

U.S. Military Presence Is Viewed as a Threat

Please tell me whether you see these activities as a threat OR NOT to the vital interests of Pakistan in the next ten years.

The US military presence in Asia

| 72 | 12 | 6 |

The US military presence in Afghanistan

| 68 | 15 | 6 |

Critical threat
Important but not critical threat
Not a threat

TAKEN FROM: WorldPublicOpinion.org and U.S. Institute of Peace, *Pakistani Public Opinion on Democracy, Islamic Militancy, and Relations with the U.S.*, January 1, 2008.

against the existential threat to Pakistani sovereignty they believe alliance with Washington entails. Most analysts contend that two December 2003 attempts to assassinate President Musharraf were carried out by Islamist militants angered by Pakistan's post-September 2001 policy shift. The "Pakistani Taliban" that has emerged in western tribal areas has sought to impose bans on television and CD players, and has instigated attacks on girls schools and nongovernmental organization-operated clinics, obstructing efforts to improve female health and education. Some observers identify a causal link between the poor state of Pakistan's public education system and the persistence of xenophobia [hatred of foreigners] and religious extremism in that country.

Anti-American sentiment is not limited to Islamic groups, however. Many across the spectrum of Pakistani society express anger at U.S. global foreign policy, in particular when such policy is perceived to be unfriendly or hostile to the Muslim world (as in, for example, Palestine and Iraq). In 2004 testimony before a Senate panel, a senior U.S. expert opined: "Pakistan is probably the most anti-American country in the world right now, ranging from the radical Islamists on one side to the liberals and Westernized elites on the other side." In a 2005 interview, President Musharraf conceded that "the man on the street [in Pakistan] does not have a good opinion of the United States." He added, by way of partial explanation, that Pakistan had been "left high and dry" after serving as a strategic U.S. ally during the 1980s. When asked about anti-American sentiment in Pakistan during his maiden July 2008 visit to the United States as head of government, Prime Minister Gillani offered that the impression in Pakistan is that "America wants war."

A Pew [Research Center] poll taken shortly before Pakistan's catastrophic October 2005 earthquake found only 23% of Pakistanis expressing a favorable view of the United States, the lowest percentage for any country surveyed. That percentage doubled to 46% in an ACNielson poll taken after large-scale U.S. disaster relief efforts in earthquake-affected areas, with the great majority of Pakistanis indicating that their perceptions had been positively influenced by witnessing such efforts. However, a January 2006 missile attack on Pakistani homes near the Afghan border killed numerous civilians and was blamed on U.S. forces, renewing animosity toward the United States among segments of the Pakistani populace. Another noteworthy episode in 2006 saw Pakistani cities hosting major public demonstrations against the publication in European newspapers of cartoons deemed offensive to Muslims. These protests, which were violent at times, included strong anti-U.S. and anti-Musharraf components, suggesting that Islamist organizers used the issue to forward their own political ends. Subsequently, a June 2006 Pew Center poll found only 27% of Pakistanis holding a favorable opinion of the United States, and this dropped to 19% in a September 2007 survey by the U.S.-based group Terror Free Tomorrow, suggesting that public diplomacy gains following the 2005 earthquake had receded.

Wide Distrust for the United States

In January 2008, the University of Maryland-based Program on International Policy Attitudes released a survey of public opinion in Pakistan. The findings indicated that significant resentment toward and distrust of the United States persist among large segments of the Pakistani public:

- 64% of Pakistanis did not trust the United States to "do the right thing in world affairs";

- more than two-thirds believed the U.S. military presence in Afghanistan is "a critical threat to Pakistan's interests";

- only 27% felt that Pakistan-U.S. security cooperation has benefitted Pakistan; and

- 86% believed that weakening and dividing the Muslim world is a U.S. goal (70% believe this is "definitely" the case). A public opinion survey conducted in June 2008 found nearly two-thirds of Pakistanis agreeing that religious extremism represented a serious problem for their country, yet less than one-third supported Pakistani army operations against religious militants in western Pakistan, and a scant 15% thought Pakistan should cooperate with the United States in its "war on terror."

Some Madrassas Encourage Militant Views

Afghanistan's Taliban movement itself began among students attending Pakistani religious schools (madrassas). Among the more than 15,000 madrassas training some 1.5 million children in Pakistan are a small percentage that have been implicated in teaching militant anti-Western, anti-American, anti-Hindu, and even anti-Shia [one of the Islamic Sects] values. Former Secretary of State [Colin] Powell once identified these as "programs that do nothing but prepare youngsters to be fundamentalists and to be terrorists." Contrary to popularly held conceptions, however, research indicates that the great majority of Pakistan's violent Islamist extremists does not emerge from the country's madrassas, but rather from the dysfunctional public school system or even from private, English-medium schools. One study found that less than one in five international terrorists sampled had Islamic education backgrounds. However, a senior leader of the secular Awami National Party that now leads a coalition government in the North West Frontier Province said in mid-2008 that many Pakistani madrassas encourage militancy and are breeding grounds for terrorism. He appealed to international donors to help Pakistan establish modern educational institutions.

Many of Pakistan's madrassas are financed and operated by Pakistani Islamist political parties such as the JUI-F (closely linked to the Taliban), as well as by multiple unknown foreign entities, many in Saudi Arabia. As many as two-thirds of the seminaries are run by the Deobandi sect, known in part for traditionally anti-Shia sentiments and at times linked to the Sipah-e-Sahaba terrorist group. In its 2007 report on international religious freedom, the U.S. State Department said, "Some unregistered and Deobandi-controlled madrassas in the FATA [Federally Administered Tribal Areas] and northern Baluchistan continued to teach extremism" and that schools run by the Jamaat al-Dawat, considered to be a front organization of the proscribed Lashkar-e-Taiba terrorist group, serve as recruitment centers for extremists. President Musharraf himself has acknowledged that a small number of seminaries were "harboring terrorists" and he has asked religious leaders to help isolate these by openly condemning them.

Global attention to Pakistan's religious schools intensified during the summer of 2005 after Pakistani officials acknowledged that suspects in London terrorist bombings visited Pakistan during the previous year and may have spent time at a madrassa near Lahore. While the Islamabad [Pakistan's capital] government repeatedly has pledged to crack down on the more extremist madrassas in his country, there continues to be little concrete evidence that it has done so. Some observers speculate that President Musharraf's alleged reluctance to enforce reform efforts was rooted in his desire to remain on good terms with Pakistan's Islamist political parties, which were seen to be an important part of his political base. When asked in late 2007 about progress in reforming the country's madrassa system, Musharraf made a rare admission of "lack of achievement," but went on to call the registration campaign and efforts to mainstream the curriculum successful.

A key aspect of madrassas' enduring appeal to Pakistani parents is the abysmal state of the country's public schools. Pakistan's primary education system ranks among the world's least effective. Congress, the Bush Administration, and the 9/11 Commission each have identified this issue as relevant to U.S. interests in South Asia. In the lead-up to Pakistan's February 2008 elections, 16 of the country's major parties committed to raising the federal education budget to 4% of GDP [gross domestic product], up from the current 2.4%. The U.S. Congress has appropriated many millions of dollars to assist Pakistan in efforts to reform its education system, including changes that would make madrassa curriculum closer in substance to that provided in non-religious schools. About $256 million has been allocated for education-related aid programs since 2002. In 2006, the U.S.-Pakistan Education dialogue was launched in Washington to bolster further engagement. In April 2008, USAID [U.S. Agency for International Development] launched a new $90 million project to bolster the effectiveness of Pakistan's public education sector. Requested funding for FY2009 includes a total of $166 million for basic and higher education programs in Pakistan.

Periodical Bibliography

M.M. Ali   "Economic Woes, Security and Political Concerns Continue to Plague Pakistan," *Washington Report on Middle East Affairs*, December 2008.

Aryn Baker   "How Pakistan Failed Itself," *Time*, May 25, 2009.

Jen Cutts   "Reading, Writing, and Radicalism?" *Maclean's*, June 1, 2009.

Economist   "Sweets and Stones," September 13, 2008.

Paul Garwood   "Pakistan, Afghanistan Look to Women to Improve Health Care," *Bulletin of the World Health Organization*, November 2006.

Adnan R. Khan   "The Last Salute," *Maclean's*, September 1, 2008.

Adnan R. Khan   "Living Like a Refugee," *Maclean's*, June 8, 2009.

Tim McGirk   "Pakistan's Other War," *Time International*, June 26, 2006.

National Review   "After Bhutto," January 28, 2008.

Nir Rosen   "Among the Allies," *Mother Jones*, January/February 2006.

Saeed Shah   "Thousands Stuck in Camps of No Return," *Observer* (London, UK), October 26, 2008.

OPPOSING
VIEWPOINTS®
SERIES

CHAPTER 2

How Can Pakistan Address Terrorism?

Chapter Preface

While Pakistan may consider India its greatest external foe, within the nation's borders the largest threat is perhaps the Taliban. By the summer of 2009, the Taliban had been behind a series of terrorist attacks that killed several thousands of Pakistanis, and efforts by the Pakistani government to reach peace deals with the Taliban have been unsuccessful. However, Pakistan did receive good news in August 2009 when the country's Taliban leader, Baitullah Mehsud, was killed by a U.S. Predator drone air strike.

According to an article published in the magazine *Foreign Policy*, a month before his death, Mehsud had led a corps of 16,000 fighters, both domestic and international, for five years. During that time, Mehsud was behind such acts as suicide bombings, taking three hundred Pakistani soldiers hostage (they were later exchanged for twenty-five imprisoned Taliban), and reportedly the assassination of former prime minister Benazir Bhutto. Mehsud had also threatened to attack Washington, D.C. Although his death prevented his threat from coming true, Mehsud and his Taliban operation were said to be responsible for 90 percent of the terrorist attacks in Pakistan, so his death should strike a serious blow for the Taliban's operations in the nation.

However, given the network of terrorists that Mehsud was able to train during his years of leadership, it may be naïve to think that the Taliban will not continue to be a threat both inside and outside Pakistan. Although Ron Moreau and Sami Yousafzai, writing for Newsweek.com, assert, "His death is a major victory for the U.S.'s war on Islamic extremists, and seriously damages the Pakistani Taliban movement," others are not so sure. Sameer Lalwani, in an essay for the New America Foundation, declares, "In the past, the Taliban have displayed surprising cohesion even after the death of senior militant commanders. In many cases, they've only been replaced by more zealous leadership."

Life in the post-Mehsud Taliban is not yet known, but that does not negate the effect that terrorism has had in Pakistan. The authors in this chapter look at how the problem of Pakistani-based terrorism can be reduced.

| *"In Pakistan today, the Taleban power expands as if without limits."*

Pakistan Must Stop the Taliban

Stephen Schwartz and Irfan Al-Alawi

In the following viewpoint, Stephen Schwartz and Irfan Al-Alawi argue that the Pakistani government is incapable of stopping the spread of the Taliban throughout its nation. The authors assert that Pakistani president Asif Ali Zardari is too willing to meet the demands of the Taliban. According to the authors, the only realistic way to stop the incursion of the Taliban is through foreign intervention, a step Zardari refuses to take. Schwartz is the executive director and Al-Alawi is the international director of the Centre for Islamic Pluralism.

As you read, consider the following questions:

1. What are the intents of Pakistani extremists, according to Schwartz and Al-Alawi?

2. As stated by the authors, how many members of the Taliban are studying in extremist schools in the Pakistani North West Frontier Province?

Stephen Schwartz and Irfan Al-Alawi, "Zardari Is Even More Afraid than Musharraf," *Spectator*, September 27, 2008. Copyright © 2008 by The Spectator. Reproduced by permission of The Spectator.

3. As explained by Schwartz and Al-Alawi, what has happened to Shia Muslims in Parachinar?

The sophisticated truck bombing of the Marriott Hotel in [Pakistan's capital] Islamabad on 20 September [2008], which took dozens of lives, was the latest incident in a campaign to destabilise the entire subcontinent. Most reports have blamed al-Qa'eda militants but the real blame for the crime belongs with the Talebanised sectors of the Pakistani armed forces and intelligence service (ISI), and the pusillanimity [cowardice] of the Pakistani president Asif Ali Zardari, widower of the assassinated Benazir Bhutto.

The Marriott assault was clearly a sequel to the bombing less than three months ago, on 7 July, at the Indian embassy in Kabul [Afghanistan], which was also devastatingly murderous. Pakistani authorities tried to deny the involvement of ISI agents, as detailed in communications intercepted by US intelligence services. Less obviously, the Taleban on both sides of the border between Afghanistan and the Pakistani North West Frontier Province (NWFP) are engaged in a full-fronted invasion of Afghanistan's eastern neighbour.

Fundamentalists Want to Radicalize Pakistan

The shift of the global Islamist terror front from Iraq to Afghanistan has less to do with opposition to the Western presence supporting [Afghani president] Hamid Karzai than is commonly supposed. The intent of the fundamentalists (claiming to act in the interest of extreme Sunnism [one Islamic sect]) is to radicalise the whole of Pakistan or, failing that, to effect a third partition of the subcontinent. Following the split between Pakistan and India in 1947, and the secession of Bangladesh (formerly East Pakistan) in 1971, the Pakistani Taleban, as the radicals are increasingly known, will settle for nothing short of full control of the NWFP.

The Pakistani Taleban could not wage war across the border were it not for the longstanding infiltration of the Pakistani army and ISI by jihadists [those espousing "holy war"]. For years, the Pakistani-Indian conflict over Kashmir was the pretext for ignoring this. Similarly, rivalry with India served as the justification for Mr Zardari's predecessor, General Pervez Musharraf, to protect Abdul Qadeer Khan, the alleged rogue physicist who we now know helped provide nuclear technology to Iran, Libya and North Korea. Zardari's rival and occasional partner, Nawaz Sharif, a recent resident of Wahhabi Saudi Arabia, continues his historic alignment with the jihadists.

Zardari insists that his government can handle the situation without foreign involvement. Such arguments are simply more rhetoric. They cover a policy of accommodation with the Taleban invaders, best exemplified when the Pakistani army fired at US helicopters on 21 September, the day after the Marriott atrocity. A week before, Pakistani forces were officially ordered to shoot at American troops if the latter crossed the barely defined Afghan border.

US leaders (including competitors in the [2008] presidential race) have also failed to understand the problem. They argue over whether Iraq or Afghanistan is more important to the anti-terror war, and note that al-Qa'eda is shifting its forces to Kabul. They assume that the collapse of jihadism in Iraq is the only reason for al-Qa'eda to refocus eastward. This is a serious mistake. The followers of [Osama] bin Laden have spent years preparing the Pakistan onslaught. We and other close observers have long argued that Pakistan, not Afghanistan, was the second most important anti-jihadist front after Iraq.

The Pakistani Government Is Incapable of Stopping the Taleban

In Pakistan today, the Taleban power expands as if without limits. The fundamentalist Deobandi sect (which gave birth to the Afghan Taleban regime, its missionary arm, Tablighi Jamaat, and the historic jihadist movement, Jama'at-e Islami) may soon be an equal counterforce to the Zardari regime. In the NWFP, the jihadist demagogue Fazlur Rahman (to whom Musharraf handed dominion over the province) is more powerful than Zardari. Mr Rahman controls many madrasas [religious schools], and we are informed that 125,000 Taleban are studying in extremist schools in the NWFP.

Not only has Mr Zardari proved himself incapable of reversing Musharraf's capitulation to the jihadists, but (to protect himself) he seems intent on satisfying their demands. He is even more afraid of the extremists than Musharraf was—this is an extraordinarily dangerous situation. Zardari and his late spouse, Benazir Bhutto, were never concerned about solving the deep problems of the country; rather, they looked to their own property and financial interests. The Bhutto-Zardari

Pakistan People's Party had as its historic slogan 'Roti, kapra, makan'—'Food, clothing, shelter'—but none of these has been delivered, and Pakistan now visibly suffers from the Third World food crisis, with reports of adulterated flour being sold in the marketplaces.

Meanwhile, the Taleban's targets are not just official political figures and Westerners. A terrible, ongoing massacre in Parachinar, administrative centre of the Kurram Agency—inside Pakistan but close to Kabul and to Tora Bora, the old bolthole of bin Laden—has gone unreported in the foreign media. Beginning last year, mass murder has descended on the Federally Administered Tribal Areas (Fata), which include Kurram, in the southwest of the NWFP. Already in 2006, according to the Pakistani ex-police officer and terrorism analyst Hassan Abbas, clashes had begun in the Fata's Khyber Agency between the Taleban and adherents of the Sufi-oriented Barelvi sect, to which the earlier, loyalist generations of subcontinental Muslim immigrants to England belonged. In the Swat district, another part of the Fata, strict sharia [Islamic] law was imposed. Christians and Sikhs were harassed. Talebanisation of the Fata also included bans on music, compulsory full covering of women and recruiting of children for suicide terror.

But Parachinar produced a special kind of horror. The Kurram Agency is surrounded on three sides by Afghanistan, and was the first refuge for bin Laden's followers after the US bombing commenced in the aftermath of 9/11 [2001]. Yet Kurram and Parachinar were inhospitable to al-Qa'eda. The Kurram Agency's half-million residents are mainly Shia Muslims—sympathetic to the Afghan Northern Alliance rather than bin Laden, and hated by the Taleban as much as non-Muslims, secular Muslims, Sufis and other non-fundamentalist Sunnis.

In the past year hundreds of Shias have been slain in the most brutal manner by the Taleban in Parachinar—their deaths accompanied by dismemberment and other brutalities.

By July of this year, ironically, the only safe road into Parachinar came from Afghanistan. The American Shia political leader Agha Shaukat Jafri insists that the jihadist elements in the ISI are as much responsible for the mass murder in Parachinar as for the Taleban invasion to the north. 'The hand of the ISI is visible wherever blood is shed in Pakistan today,' Jafri said. But calls for a clean-up in the intelligence organisation have been ignored for years.

Two Ways to Defeat the Taleban

There seem to be only two options for defeating the Pakistani Taleban. One, a unification of all moderate Muslim factions, appears utopian. The other is simpler and more realistic, but rejected by Zardari on the grounds that Western intervention in Afghanistan and US involvement with Pakistan already contribute to the influence of the radicals. That is foreign military action, uniting the US with NATO [North Atlantic Treaty Organization] and other forces, to restore some semblance of the stability that first Musharraf and later Zardari have let slip away.

> "The terrorists are not, so to speak, from [President Asif Ali Zardari's] part of the country; and there seems little he can do about them."

Pakistan Must Take Action to End Terrorist Attacks on India

Global Agenda

In the following viewpoint, Global Agenda asserts that militant groups based in Pakistan are the likely culprits behind the November 2008 terrorist attacks in Mumbai, India. The magazine argues that because India cannot respond as strongly as it might wish to, it is the responsibility of Pakistan's government to stop the terrorists. However, the president of Pakistan does not have enough power over the parts of the country where the terrorist groups live or over the military-intelligence organizations that support these groups. Global Agenda is a publication of the World Economic Forum.

As you read, consider the following questions:

1. Which militant group do India's leaders blame for the attacks on Mumbai, according to the magazine?

2. As explained by *Global Agenda*, what are the two obstacles preventing India from mounting a strong response to Pakistan?

3. How has Pakistan's president reached out to India, as detailed by the magazine?

It may have been a slip of the tongue. But there was something very revealing about a remark that Pakistan's president, Asif Ali Zardari, made in an interview with an Indian television channel on November 30th [2008]. Asked about allegations that Pakistan was involved in the murderous onslaught on Mumbai, he promised, before the world, strict action "if any evidence points towards any individual or group in my part of the country".

The (perhaps unintended) implication that Mr Zardari is in control of only part of Pakistan is all too true. And that helps explain why it is so difficult for India to respond.

A Possible Pakistani Link Behind the Bombings

India's leaders seem convinced—and American intelligence officials reportedly concur—that there was some Pakistani involvement in the attack.

Specifically, they blame Lashkar-e-Taiba, which along with Jaish-e-Mohammad was one of the two most notorious militant groups set up with the connivance and help of Pakistan's military-intelligence outfit, Inter-Services Intelligence (ISI), to help wage an insurgency against Indian rule in the part of Kashmir it controls. These groups now seem allied with a broader jihadist ["holy war"] movement along the Afghan-Pakistani frontier.

The groups are alleged to have been behind—or at least lent a helping hand in—a series of bloody attacks on India: the attempt in 2001 to kill India's leaders in a raid on parliament in Delhi; the bombing in 2003 of parts of Mumbai, in-

Pakistan Must Work with India to Fight Terrorism

The British government urged India to send its troops to Afghanistan [to join] the war against terror. [The] government should consider doing this only if Pakistan sincerely accepts joint operations with India. A start could be made against terrorist training camps located in Pakistan. Coordinated operations should be undertaken in all terrorist spots. . . . Only then would joint operations inside Afghanistan succeed. Clearly such operations would have to be accompanied by a dialogue with both the Pashtuns and Kashmiri separatists. To meet their respective aspirations India and Pakistan would first have to evolve a future roadmap for South Asia.

Rajinder Puri, "Who Needs America?
India-Pakistan Must Jointly Combat Terrorism,"
www.boloji.com.

cluding the Taj Mahal hotel, a target in the latest attack; the even bigger slaughter entailed in the coordinated bombing of Mumbai's commuter rail-network in July 2006.

The first of those attacks, the assault on parliament, initially seemed to threaten all-out war. India mobilised its troops to go to the border. Foreign governments advised their citizens to avoid the subcontinent. Public opinion in both countries became alarmingly bellicose [hostile].

America, however, did not want Indo-Pakistani tension to distract Pakistan from the war on its other frontier, with Afghanistan. It put pressure on Pervez Musharraf, then Pakistan's president, who banned the two militant groups. But they survived under different names and continued to sow violence in Kashmir and elsewhere.

Yet in 2003 when Atal Behari Vajpayee, then India's prime minister, made friendly overtures to Pakistan, it seemed hugely popular in both countries.

Since then, when figurative Pakistani fingerprints have been found all over terrorist attacks on Indian soil, huge efforts were made not to let them derail the peace process Mr Vajpayee set in train. Promises of anti-terrorist co-operation were made; a joint commission was set up; and a gradual thawing of relations continued regardless.

By attacking India's commercial hub and luxury hotels where many foreigners stay, the latest atrocity was designed to cause maximum damage to India's image. It pushes India's remarkable forbearance to its limits.

A Challenge for India to Respond to Pakistan

But there are two huge obstacles to India's mounting a robust response. First, to the extent that the attackers can be said to have anything that can be dignified with the name of a strategy, it must be to provoke just the sort of confrontation that followed the 2001 raid on parliament. Pakistan has already said it would move troops to its frontier with India if need be. That would ease pressure on the Taliban and their allies on the other border.

Second, there is the problem Mr Zardari alluded to. There are large swathes of Pakistan where his writ does not run [his authority carries no weight]—notably in the tribal areas, but even in parts of the North-West Frontier Province.

And he is a civilian president. It is not certain the army or the ISI will follow his orders unquestioningly. An early promise to send the ISI's chief to Delhi [India's capital] turned out to be a "miscommunication".

Moreover, it does not seem in India's interests to weaken Mr Zardari. Politically shaky at home, he has been reaching out to India; calling militants in Kashmir "terrorists", promising no first-use of Pakistan's nuclear arsenal, urging bigger commercial links, and insisting that terrorists are his enemy as much as India's.

The trouble is, the terrorists are not, so to speak, from his part of the country; and there seems little he can do about them—even if, as seems likely, he wants them roundly defeated.

> "The Pakistani military-intelligence community has never made the fundamental decision to turn its back on the culture of jihad."

Pakistani Terrorism Complicates a Troubled Relationship with India

Ramesh Thakur

Terrorist attacks on Mumbai, India, show that India and Pakistan should not be viewed as similar by the world community, asserts Ramesh Thakur in the following viewpoint. According to Thakur, the attacks showed the world that India is one of the biggest victims of terrorism while Pakistan's government has been both unable and unwilling to stop the terrorist networks inside its borders. Thakur concludes that Pakistan-based terrorist groups, which are a threat to India and the rest of the world, must be eliminated. Thakur is the director of the Balsillie School of International Affairs in Waterloo, Ontario.

Ramesh Thakur, "There Is No Moral Equivalence," *Globe and Mail*, December 11, 2008, p. A17. Copyright © 2008 Globe Interactive, a division of Bell Globemedia Publishing, Inc. Reproduced by permission.

As you read, consider the following questions:

1. How many people in India are killed by terrorist attacks each year, as stated by Thakur?

2. In Thakur's view, what has overshadowed Pakistan's president's overtures to India?

3. In the author's view, what will be the consequence if the structure of Pakistani terrorism is not destroyed completely?

India reflexively blames Pakistan for nearly all terrorist incidents; Islamabad [Pakistan's capital] habitually denies any involvement or links. After last month's [November 2008] attacks in Mumbai, however, the proper response to Pakistani denials is the double positive of "yeah, right." For all of India's mistakes, abuses and atrocities in Kashmir, the worst outcome would be for outsiders to impose a moral equivalence between democratic India and Pakistan.

A New View of Lashkar-e-Taiba

According to U.S. officials quoted by the *New York Times*, Pakistan's notorious Inter-Services Intelligence [ISI] agency has shared intelligence with and provided protection to the banned Lashkar-e-Taiba [LET]. Meanwhile, India has been second only to Iraq as the stage for terrorism, averaging more than 1,000 killings annually for the past four years.

But even by these standards, the carnage in Mumbai stands out for its savagery and audacity. The combination of training, selection and advance reconnaissance of targets, diversionary tactics, discipline, munitions, cryptographic communications and false identifications is typically associated with special-forces units. Previous terrorist methods had involved remote controlled or timed devices, but this was a three-stage amphibious operation.

After Mumbai, even U.S. agencies are reassessing their view of Lashkar-e-Taiba, concluding it is a more capable and

Pakistan's Government Has Allowed Attacks on India

There is a clear distinction between the terrorist attacks within Pakistan, which are led mostly by the al Qaeda and the Pakistani Taliban that are annoyed with the country's alliance with the United States, and the terrorist targeting of India by jihadi ["holy war"] outfits like the LeT [Lashkar-e-Taiba] and the Jaish-e-Mohammad. The latter continue to enjoy patronage of the Pakistan Army and the ISI [Inter-Services Intelligence] and their operations have never been disrupted either during Pervez Musharraff's reign or under the present civilian government.

Shanthie Mariet D'Souza,
"The Pakistan Link to the Mumbai Terror Attacks,"
December 5, 2008, www.idsa.in.

greater threat than previously believed. For the first time in India, luxury hotels, a hospital and a Jewish centre were attacked and foreigners and Indians were killed without discrimination. This is also the first major terrorist attack in India that received saturation coverage by the world news media, bringing home to Westerners that India is a front-line state against international terrorism.

Pakistan's Government Has Been Ineffective

Many Indians are as angry and disgusted with their own politicians as with Pakistan's perfidy [breach of trust]. New Delhi's intelligence failures and bumbling response, worthy of Inspector Clouseau [the bumbling detective in the *Pink Panther* series], were amplified by some politicians' tone-deaf comments, which reeked of insolence and imperiousness.

Most Indian officials have parsed their words more carefully, however, pointing to "elements" inside Pakistan—a recognition of rogue factions within Inter-Services Intelligence. Fareed Zakaria, a Mumbai-born Muslim, has written of Pakistan's civilian government being "an innocent bystander" as known terrorist groups operate with brazen openness.

President Asif Ali Zardari's overtures of friendship to New Delhi have been overshadowed by his ineffectualness against the military-intelligence-terrorists complex. He agreed to an Indian request for the head of the ISI to travel to India to help co-ordinate the investigation, but reneged when the military and intelligence officers balked—the foreign-affairs equivalent of a soccer "own goal." To the extent that terror networks are regionalized across South Asia, so should counterterrorism networks be regionally co-ordinated.

Pakistan Must Rein in Terrorism

U.S. Secretary of State Condoleezza Rice and American intelligence sources have made clear they share Indian assessments of Pakistan's role in terrorism against India. The goal of pro-militant ISI agents may be to provoke Indian troop movements and draw Pakistani units from the Afghan border region to Kashmir, to show the civilian government that the military still calls the shots and to restore the agency as custodian of national interests rather than a stooge of the Americans. Sensitive to these strategic calculations, India has demonstrated extraordinary forbearance and restraint. This must be matched by credible, effective and visible action by Pakistan to rein in the terrorists and those with financial, organizational and personnel links to them.

Such action is not likely without sustained and intense international pressure, because the Pakistani military-intelligence community has never made the fundamental decision to turn its back on the culture of jihad ["holy war"]. Lashkar-e-Taiba is believed to have been complicit in the 2001 attack on India's

Parliament and the 2006 Mumbai train blasts. Every time Pakistan comes under intense international pressure, a few terrorist suspects are captured and jailed. Islamabad denied for years that LET had morphed into the "charitable" Jamaat-ud-Dawa with its leader living openly in Lahore, but—surprise, surprise—when Western pressure was ratcheted up after Mumbai, camps were raided and some radicals were captured.

This should no longer be enough. The entire structure of Pakistani terrorism must be verifiably destroyed to international satisfaction, on pain of the country being labelled a terrorist state under United Nations resolutions. Otherwise, the price will be paid increasingly not just by Indian victims, but by Western ones. If Kashmir was the sole motivating force of the Mumbai terrorists, they would have spared the foreign victims. Indeed, they were equally cruel to Indian Muslims, rich guests and poor workers. Their agenda stands exposed by their own choice of victims.

For the terrorists to be destroyed as a potent force for evil, their links with Pakistan's military and intelligence must be severed, completely and irreversibly. For this to happen, Pakistan's military and intelligence elite must learn to construct their national interest differently. To help or push them to do so, the international community and the world's media must cease and desist from hyphenating India with Pakistan.

> *"Part of the problem for India is that it has very few realistic options for dealing with Pakistan."*

India Does Not Blame Pakistan's Civilian Leadership for Terrorist Attacks

Andrew Buncombe

India recognizes that the Pakistani government is not behind the terrorist attacks on Mumbai, Andrew Buncombe opines in the following viewpoint. However, he argues, the Indian government is trying to keep pressure on Pakistan to address the problem of militant groups within the Pakistani borders. According to Buncombe, the best way for India and Pakistan to resolve this issue and avoid war is through international pressure from the United States, China, and Saudi Arabia. Buncombe is The Independent's Asia correspondent.

As you read, consider the following questions:

1. Why has India changed its approach toward Pakistan, in Buncombe's view?

Andrew Buncombe, "The Big Question: Is India Right to Blame Pakistan for the Attacks on Mumbai?" *The Independent on Sunday*, January 7, 2009. Copyright © 2009 Independent Newspapers (UK) Ltd. Reproduced by permission.

2. According to the author, why can't India launch a military strike in Pakistan?

3. What are the three reasons given by Buncombe as to why the attacks on Mumbai could lead to war between India and Pakistan?

In recent days the Indian government has stepped up the war of words with Pakistan that started when terror attacks in Mumbai left about 170 people dead. Yesterday [January 6, 2009], in his most outspoken statement yet, the Indian Prime Minister Manmohan Singh said Pakistan authorities "must have" been involved in the terror attack in November [2008]. Though not accusing the government in Islamabad [Pakistan's capital] directly, he continued: "There is enough evidence to show that, given the sophistication and military precision of the attack, it must have had the support of some official agencies in Pakistan."

What was Pakistan's response?

While Mr Singh's comments were not particularly different from those made in recent days by the country's Foreign Secretary and Home Minister, the response in Pakistan was especially angry—possibly because they came from the Prime Minister himself. Officials in Islamabad dismissed the comments as a "propaganda offensive" and said that claiming state agencies were involved in the attacks was both unwarranted and unacceptable. "India must refrain from hostile propaganda, and must not whip up tensions," said a Foreign Ministry statement. "Pakistan emphatically rejects the unfortunate allegations."

India Has Changed Its Rhetoric

Does India believe that the civilian government is behind the attacks?

Almost certainly not. Indian officials have stressed they are not pointing fingers at Pakistan's civilian leadership, headed by the President Asif Ali Zardari and the Prime Minister Yousaf Gilani. Until this point they have also been careful to draw a distinction between so-called "state actors" and "non-state" actors. These comments suggest, however, they believe that some elements of Pakistan's state—the intelligence agencies for example—may have been involved. On Monday [January 5, 2009] India's Foreign Secretary, Shivshankar Menon, went as far as to say: "Even the so-called non-state actors function within a state are citizens of a state. We don't think there's such a thing as non-state actors."

So why has their approach changed?

India is determined to keep up the pressure on Pakistan. Its shift in rhetoric coincides with the passing to Pakistan of a dossier [collection of documents] of evidence it says proves the attacks were carried out by Pakistan-based militants— members of the banned group Lashkar-e-Taiba (LeT). The dossier reportedly included transcripts of electronic intercepts and interrogation reports from the questioning of Mohammed Ajmal Kasab, the sole surviving militant. Some reports claim the dossier contained information detailing strict instructions given by the militants' handlers to those who carried out the attacks, stressing the need to "kill Jews" and to seize a senior Indian official. Indian officials said taken in its entirety, the evidence "leads to the conclusion that the plot was hatched in Pakistan and as the operation in Mumbai was on, it was masterminded and controlled from Pakistan".

Is there more to it?

Part of the problem for India is that it has very few realistic options for dealing with Pakistan. Officials in Delhi [India's capital] know that if they were to launch any sort of military strike against suspected terror targets inside Pakistan, the result could be devastating; the civilian government in Pakistan would be weakened; there would be huge public anger in the country and there would almost certainly be more attacks launched on Indian targets as a result. In such circumstances,

India can realistically do little more than speak firmly and seek to keep international support on its side. It's also worth bearing in mind that, with an election scheduled to take place in the next couple of months, Indian officials—in much the same way as their Pakistan counterparts—need to speak differently for different audiences. The Congress Party-led government has often been accused by its main opposition rival, the BJP [Bharatiya Janata Party], of being soft on terrorism and in the aftermath of Mumbai, Mr Singh and his senior ministers want to be seen to be acting firmly. It may also reflect a belief in Delhi that the Indian government needs to address different power centres in Pakistan—the civilian administration, the military and the intelligence establishment.

Pakistan's Position Is Fragile

What steps has Pakistan taken so far?

In the aftermath of the attacks, Pakistan made warm, cooperative noises and arrested about 50 people associated with LeT and closed down a number of its facilities. Mr Zardari even offered to send the head of the ISI [Inter-Services Intelligence] agency to India to help, though this was quickly overruled by the military. Since then it appears to have dug its heels in, insisting that intelligence suggesting the involvement of Pakistan-based militants it had been given through second parties, including the US and Britain, was not conclusive. Even now, while it says it is reviewing the dossier of evidence it has been given directly, officials have raised doubts about its veracity or completeness. It has also said it would not extradite any alleged suspects to India, as no treaty exists for such procedures.

Could Pakistan do more?

The problem for Mr Zardari and the civilian government that has held office for less than a year, is that its position is terribly fragile. Mr Zardari faces challenges on many fronts, and how far the military would allow the government to move

Doubts About the Perpetrators of the Mumbai Bombing

Approximately 3,500 men and women in Pakistan were asked, "Terrorists recently attacked the city of Mumbai, killing 164 people. The news is reporting that the attacks were planned in Pakistan and carried out by Lashkar-e-Taiba. Do you believe this is true?"

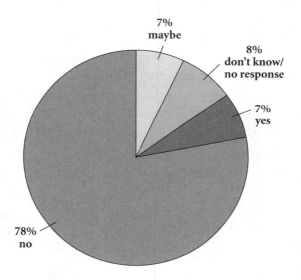

7%
maybe

8%
don't know/
no response

7%
yes

78%
no

TAKEN FROM: International Republican Institute, "Pakistan Public Opinion Survey," March 7–30, 2009.

against militants such as the LeT, with which it may still retain links, is unclear. While the president may wish to be seen to cooperate with the international community, there are vast domestic pressures not to be seen to bow towards India, a historic adversary.

How significant are their historical disagreements?

All-important. India and Pakistan have fought on three occasions. They faced off with each other in 2002 when some analysts believed the nuclear-armed countries were again heading for war. As a result there is observable mutual distrust and even the most level-headed of officials often betray seemingly illogical suspicion of the other side. The media in both countries has sometimes been guilty of nationalistic or hysterical coverage.

What are the chances of a joint investigation?

India is nervous of sharing too much intelligence with Pakistan and the ISI, elements of which were blamed by Delhi and Washington for involvement in a bomb attack last year [2008] on the Indian Embassy in Kabul that left more than 50 people dead. That may be why India took so long to directly provide Pakistan with the dossier of evidence. At the moment there are several concurrent and separate investigations being carried out by India, the ISI, the FBI [U.S. Federal Bureau of Investigation] and Scotland Yard [Britain's Metropolitan Police].

What offers the best hope of resolving things?

India is hopeful that international pressure from the US, China and Saudi Arabia—which have the most influence over Pakistan—might elicit a further response from Islamabad, in whose court the ball now lies since being handed the dossier. Joe Biden, the Vice-President elect, will this week [January 2009] be the latest US envoy to visit Pakistan for talks to defuse the tension. If Pakistan were to try and prosecute some LeT members, India could at least claim some sort of result. It will also, of course, have to address the issue of those Indians allegedly also involved in the plot.

War Is a Possibility

Could the nuclear-armed neighbours come to blows over Mumbai?

Yes. . .

- The two nations have already fought three times before.

- Both sides have dispatched thousands of troops to their border. This cannot help but raise tensions.

- There is widespread mistrust and suspicion from both parties about each other and no sense that these suspicions can be easily allayed.

No . . .

- The international community wants Pakistan to focus on the militants in the tribal areas who attack Western troops in Afghanistan.

- Military action by India could lead to a military coup in Pakistan.

- Both sides are all too well aware of the huge cost, human and financial, of conflict.

| "Al Qaeda has regenerated its ability to attack the United States and succeeded in establishing a safe haven in Pakistan's FATA."

The United States Has Failed to Address the Problem of Terrorism in Pakistan

U.S. Government Accountability Office

In the following viewpoint, the U.S. Government Accountability Office (GAO) maintains that the U.S. government has failed to destroy the terrorist threat that has developed in Pakistan's Federally Administered Tribal Areas (FATA). The GAO explains that Al Qaeda has secured a safe haven in Pakistan, where it trains operatives for attacks across the globe. According to the GAO, the United States has relied too much on the Pakistani military to end this threat, rather than developing a comprehensive plan that includes elements such as diplomatic and development assistance, along with law enforcement support. The GAO is a nonpartisan agency that works on behalf of Congress by investigating how federal funds are spent.

U.S. Government Accountability Office, "Combating Terrorism: The United States Lacks Comprehensive Plan to Destroy the Terrorist Threat and Close the Safe Haven in Pakistan's Federally Administered Tribal Areas," April 2008, pp. 9–13.

As you read, consider the following questions:

1. According to the GAO, how much aid has the United States given to Pakistan between 2002 and 2007?

2. What was the conclusion of the 2008 *Annual Threat Assessment*, as stated by the author?

3. As explained by the GAO, why has the United States relied on Pakistan's military?

The United States has not met its national security goals to destroy the terrorist threat and close the safe haven in the FATA [Federally Administered Tribal Areas], despite more than $10.5 billion in U.S. support to Pakistan since 2002. Various national security strategies have called for the use of all elements of national power, such as diplomatic, military, intelligence, development assistance, economic, and law enforcement support, to meet these goals; however, the United States has relied principally on supporting the Pakistani military to meet these goals. According to [the departments of] Defense and State, the Pakistani government deployed up to 120,000 military and paramilitary forces to combat terrorism in the FATA. Despite this effort, the 2007 NIE [National Intelligence Estimate], State and embassy documents, and Defense and State officials, including those operating in Pakistan, have concluded that al Qaeda has regenerated its ability to attack the United States and succeeded in establishing a safe haven in Pakistan's FATA.

Pakistan Is a Safe Haven for al Qaeda

On October 1, 2007, State provided Congress with a report in response to a requirement in the Implementation of the 9/11 Commission Act of 2007 (9/11 Commission Act). The report stated that it had determined that Pakistan was (1) committed to eliminating from Pakistani territory any organization, such as the Taliban, al Qaeda, or any successor engaged in military, insurgent, or terrorist activities in Afghanistan; (2) undertaking a comprehensive military, legal, economic, and political campaign to achieve the goal described; and (3) making demonstrated, significant, and sustained progress toward eliminating support or safe havens for terrorists. Notwithstanding State's report to Congress, we found broad agreement that al Qaeda had established a safe haven in the FATA and reconstituted its attack capability. In particular, the unclassified versions of the 2007 NIE and 2008 *Annual Threat Assessment* state that al Qaeda has regenerated its attack capability and secured a safe haven in Pakistan's FATA. These conclusions are supported by a broad array of sources, including Defense, State, and senior U.S. embassy officials in Pakistan.

The NIE and other sources have found that al Qaeda has established a safe haven in Pakistan. The [Director of National Intelligence] DNI's 2008 assessment stated that the safe haven in Pakistan provides al Qaeda with many of the same advantages it had when it was based across the border in Afghanistan. According to the assessment, the safe haven in the FATA serves as a staging area for al Qaeda's attacks in support of the Taliban in Afghanistan. Further, it serves as a location for training new terrorist operatives for attacks in Pakistan, the Middle East, Africa, Europe, and the United States. U.S. government officials in Washington and Pakistan also acknowledge that al Qaeda has established a safe haven near Pakistan's border with Afghanistan. For example, State's April 2007 *Country Reports on Terrorism* states that Pakistan remains a major source of Islamic extremism and a safe haven for some top terrorist leaders, including those of al Qaeda.

The NIE, *The Terrorist Threat to the U.S. Homeland,* also found that al Qaeda had effectively found replacements for many of its senior operational planners over the years. The NIE stated that, in the past 2 years, al Qaeda's central leadership regenerated the core operational capabilities needed to conduct attacks against the United States. It also found that al

Qaeda's central leadership, based in the border area of Pakistan, is and will remain the most serious terrorist threat to the United States.

Al Qaeda's Resurgence Threatens U.S. National Security

The 2008 DNI *Annual Threat Assessment* and other sources have concluded that the resurgence of al Qaeda terrorists on the border between Pakistan and Afghanistan now pose a preeminent threat to U.S. national security. The assessment also examines the impact of not meeting the national security goals. It states that al Qaeda is now using the Pakistani safe haven to put the last element necessary to launch another attack against America into place, including the identification, training, and positioning of Western operatives for an attack. It stated that al Qaeda is most likely using the FATA to plot terrorist attacks against political, economic, and infrastructure targets in America "designed to produce mass casualties, visually dramatic destruction, significant economic aftershocks, and/or fear among the population."

DNI's 2008 assessment found that al Qaeda and other Pakistan-based militants now also pose a threat to Pakistan. The assessment found an unparalleled increase in suicide attacks against Pakistan's military and civilians over the past year, with total casualties in 2007 exceeding all such attacks in the preceding 5 years. These attacks were ordered by Pakistan-based militants, many of whom are allied with al Qaeda. It found that the terrorist assassination of former Prime Minister Benazir Bhutto could encourage terrorists to strike the Pakistani establishment anywhere in the country. The assessment concluded that radical elements now have the potential to undermine Pakistan itself.

U.S. Funding Focuses on the Military

Since 2002, the United States has relied principally on the Pakistani military to address U.S. national security goals in the

Percentage of U.S. Funding Directed toward Military, Border Security, and Development Activities in Pakistan's FATA and Border Region from Fiscal Years 2002 to 2007

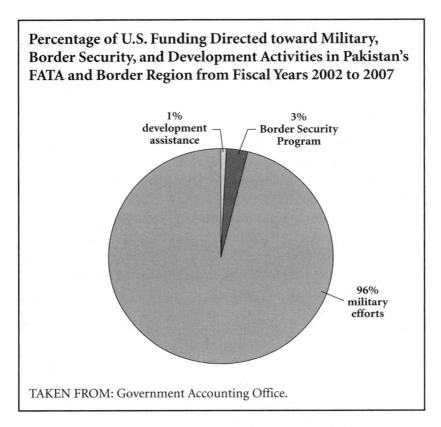

1%
development
assistance

3%
Border Security
Program

96%
military
efforts

TAKEN FROM: Government Accounting Office.

FATA. There have been limited efforts, however, to address other underlying causes of terrorism in the FATA, such as providing development assistance or addressing the FATA's political needs. For example, although the FATA has some of the worst development indicators in Pakistan and is ruled under colonial administrative and legal structures dating from 1901, the United States has devoted little funding to address these issues in the FATA.

From fiscal years 2002 to 2007, the United States has provided Pakistan with more than $10.5 billion in funds and assistance. Approximately $5.8 billion of this amount has been directed at efforts to combat terrorism in Pakistan's FATA and the border region. About 96 percent of this amount was used to reimburse the Pakistani government through CSF [Coalition Support Funds] for military operations in support of Operation Enduring Freedom in Afghanistan, most significantly against terrorists in Pakistan's FATA and border region. We identified only two nonmilitary activities that occured in the FATA and border region: State's Border Security Program, which received about $187 million, and USAID [U.S. Agency for International Development] development activities, which amounted to about $40 million.

According to a State Department report, Pakistan's military forces have had some tactical successes in the FATA. The Pakistani government stationed military and paramilitary forces along the border with Afghanistan, and security operations in the FATA disrupted terrorist activity by targeting and raiding al Qaeda and other militant safe havens. According to State, Pakistan has helped kill or capture hundreds of suspected terrorists, including al Qaeda operatives and Taliban leaders. In addition, Pakistani military operations have resulted in the deaths of approximately 1,400 members of its security forces.

The U.S. Needs a More Comprehensive Plan to Fight Terrorism

Defense, State, U.S. embassy, and Pakistani government officials recognize that relying primarily on the Pakistani military has not succeeded in neutralizing al Qaeda and preventing the establishment of a safe haven in the FATA. State's April 2007 *Country Reports on Terrorism* states that, despite having Pakistani troops in the FATA and sustaining hundreds of casualties, the government of Pakistan has been unable to exert control over the area. The report concluded that Pakistan has now recognized that military operations alone will not restore security and stability to the FATA. Similarly, U.S. embassy officials in Pakistan stated that Taliban and al Qaeda elements have created a safe haven in the FATA and have used it to plan and launch attacks on Afghan, Pakistani, U.S., and coalition forces in Afghanistan and Pakistan. The embassy further noted that al Qaeda and the Taliban continue to recruit, train, and operate in the FATA.

According to senior embassy officials, U.S. reliance on Pakistan's military stemmed from the lack of a comprehensive plan to guide embassy efforts and the sense that the Pakistani military was the most capable institution in Pakistan to quickly undertake operations against al Qaeda immediately after the attacks of 9/11. Senior embassy officials stated that this may have led to an "over-reliance" on the Pakistani military to achieve U.S. national security objectives in Pakistan.

Despite the recognition of U.S. government officials, including the U.S. President and Congress, that a comprehensive plan employing all elements of national power—diplomatic, military, intelligence, development assistance, economic, and law enforcement support—was needed to combat terrorism and close the terrorist safe haven in Pakistan's FATA region, a comprehensive plan to meet U.S. national security goals in the region was never developed. Recognizing in 2006 that military efforts alone would not succeed in the FATA, the embassy, with Defense, State, and USAID support, and in conjunction with the Pakistani government in power at that time, began an effort to focus more attention on the other key elements of national power, such as development and public diplomacy, to address U.S. national security goals in the FATA. However, this effort has not been formally approved by U.S. government stakeholders who would play a key role in the funding and implementation of such an effort, and support from the recently elected Pakistani government is uncertain.

> *"There can be no justification for Pakistan carrying out human rights violations including arbitrary arrest, secret and unlawful detention and enforced disappearances."*

Pakistan Must Stop Violating Human Rights in Its Fight Against Terrorism

Amnesty International

Pakistan's efforts to cooperate with the United States and end terrorism in its borders does not give it the right to engage in a variety of human rights abuses, Amnesty International argues in the following viewpoint. Among the abuses detailed by the organization are enforced disappearances, torture, and arbitrary arrests. However, the organization points out, these tactics have failed to effectively address the power held by both Pakistan's army and the Taliban in the nation's tribal areas. Amnesty International is a worldwide organization that campaigns on behalf of human rights.

Amnesty International, *Pakistan: Human Rights Ignored in the 'War on Terror*,' September 2006. Reproduced by permission.

As you read, consider the following questions:

1. According to Amnesty International, how many people are on Pakistan's death row?

2. As quoted by the organization, what does Article 4 of the Constitution of Pakistan state?

3. How many madrassas were registered as of February 2006, as stated by Amnesty International?

"I cannot believe that there can be a trade between the effective fight against terrorism and the protection of civil liberties. If as individuals we are asked to give up our freedom, our liberties, our human rights, as protection against terrorism, do we in the end have protection?"

UN Secretary-General Kofi Annan, September 2006.

In its pursuit of the US-led "war on terror", the Pakistani government has committed numerous violations of human rights protected in the Constitution of Pakisian and in international human rights law. They include the right to life and the security of the person; to be free from torture and other cruel, inhuman or degrading treatment or punishment (ill-treatment); to be free from enforced disappearance and to challenge the lawfulness of detention. Victims of human rights violations in the "war on terror" include Pakistani and non-Pakistani terror suspects, men and some women, children of terror suspects, sometimes held as hostages, journalists who have reported on the "war on terror" and medical personnel who allegedly treated terror suspects.

Human Rights Are Dismal in Pakistan

Irrespective of the "war on terror", the people of Pakistan suffer widespread violations of their civil and political rights. In Pakistan, torture and ill-treatment are endemic; arbitrary and unlawful arrest and detention are a growing problem; extrajudicial executions of criminal suspects are frequent; well over

7,000 people are on death row and there has recently been a wave of executions. Discriminatory laws deny the basic human rights of women and of minority groups.

To this dismal human rights record, Pakistan's actions in the "war on terror" have added a further layer of violations. Hundreds of people suspected of links to al-Qa'ida or the Taleban have been arbitrarily arrested and detained. Scores have become victims of enforced disappearance; some of these have been unlawfully transferred (sometimes in return for money) to the custody of other countries, notably the USA.

Many people have been detained incommunicado in undisclosed places of detention and tortured or ill-treated. Their families, distressed about the lack of information on the whereabouts and fate of their loved ones, have been harassed and threatened when seeking information. The right to habeas corpus [prisoner's right to challenge the terms of his incarceration before a judge] has been systematically undermined as state agents have refused to comply with court directions or have lied in court.

The fate of some of the victims of arbitrary arrest, detention and enforced disappearance has been disclosed—some have been charged with criminal offences unrelated to terrorism, others have been released without charge, reportedly after being warned to keep quiet about their experience, while some have been found dead. However, many have been unlawfully transferred to other countries, without any judicial or other procedures, and in violation of the principle of *non-refoulement*, which prohibits people being sent to countries where they face serious human rights abuses. Some were transferred to US custody and have ended up in the US Naval Base at Guantánamo Bay (Cuba), Bagram airbase (Afghanistan) or secret detention centres elsewhere. Others have been unlawfully returned to their countries of origin, where they may be at risk of further abuse. However, many remain unaccounted for—their fate and whereabouts are unknown.

The clandestine nature of the arrest and detention of terror suspects makes it impossible to ascertain exactly how many people have been subjected to arbitrary detention or enforced disappearance. The independent non-governmental organisation, the Pak Institute for Peace Studies in May 2006 stated that over 1,000 people have been arrested in the "war on terror" in Pakistan. US President George W Bush has said on several occasions that "our ally, Pakistan, has killed or captured more than 600 terrorists". Pakistan President Pervez Musharraf has mentioned some 700 terror suspects arrested, but these figures may not be accurate.

Society Is Indifferent to the Problems in Pakistan

Amnesty International is concerned that there has been no public outcry against the erosion of human rights reported in Pakistan as a result of its involvement in the "war on terror". Civil society, political parties and the media have by and large ignored the issue. People who have taken up the issue have been subjected to harassment, threats and abuse. Journalists have told Amnesty International that there is a perception in Pakistani civil society that those people who have been subjected to arbitrary detention and enforced disappearance belong to Islamist groups that support terrorist activities, sectarian killings and discriminatory laws and practices.

Amnesty International is concerned about the increase in human rights violations in Pakistan in the context of the "war on terror" and the apparent indifference to this in society. Human rights are universal and should be enjoyed by all. Amnesty International takes no position on the guilt or innocence of alleged terror suspects; however, the organisation insists that everyone must be able to enjoy the full range of human rights. The rights to life, the security of the person, the protection of law and to freedom from torture cannot be suspended in any circumstances. Article 4 of the Constitution of Pakistan provides that "to enjoy the protection of law and to be treated in accordance with law is the inalienable right of every citizen, wherever he may be, and of every other person for the time being in Pakistan". These words must become a reality, including in the context of the "war on terror".

The practice of enforced disappearance, which was rare before 2001, has become more common in contexts besides the "war on terror". Over the past two years, dozens of Baloch nationalists are believed to have been subjected to enforced disappearance and there are recent reports that leaders of Sindhi parties and members of the Shia minority have as well. The increasing frequency of such human rights violations and the impunity enjoyed by the perpetrators may also have contributed to raising the threshold of tolerance to human rights violations generally in Pakistan. The non-governmental Human Rights Commission of Pakistan (HRCP), in its annual report for 2004, said that the "tone of media reports [about deaths in custody] did not reveal the feeling of outrage that used to be noticed in reports of such incidents in the past". It said that this might be attributable to the "impact of the war on terrorism on the public psyche" and that "people were getting used to deaths in custody as *normal happenings*".

Amnesty International fully recognizes the right and duty of the Pakistani authorities to prevent and punish crimes, including violent crimes such as acts of terrorism, and to bring to justice those responsible for committing such crimes. The organisation has consistently denounced indiscriminate attacks and attacks targeting civilians carried out by armed groups such as al-Qai'da. Specifically, the organisation has condemned the attacks on the USA on 11 September 2001 as crimes against humanity. All those responsible for these and similar crimes must be brought to justice. At the same time, measures taken to combat terrorism must respect national human rights guaranteed under national and international law. There can be no justification for Pakistan carrying out human rights violations including arbitrary arrest, secret and unlawful detention and enforced disappearances; torture and other ill-treatment; extrajudicial executions; and unlawful transfers to other countries in violation of the principle of *non-refoulement* and in circumvention of Pakistan's extradition law.

Pakistan As an American Ally

Pakistan's cooperation with the USA in the "war on terror" has meant that it has provided logistics facilities, shared intelligence and has arrested and handed over terror suspects. US Lieutenant General Karl Eikenberry, Commander of the Combined Forces Command Afghanistan stated recently, "if you look at Pakistan's actions over the past several years, Pakistan has arrested and killed more Al Qaeda members than any other country. Pakistan is a great ally in the war on terror".

The Pakistani government has after September 2001 also banned Islamist organisations, many of which are widely believed to have close links to al-Qa'ida and the Taleban. It has frozen bank accounts suspected of belonging to militant organisations, condemned hate-speech and literature calling for violence and announced reforms of the *madrassa* [religious school] system. In return the USA has written off debts, extended substantial grants and reinstated arms sales and a military training programme earlier suspended.

Domestically, the government's pursuit of the "war on terror" has met with resistance, particularly from Islamic groups. The *Muttahida Majlis-e-Amal* (MMA), an alliance of six Islamic parties, for the first time gained a significant parliamentary presence in general elections in October 2002 on an anti-US platform. It formed the provincial governments in the North West Frontier Province (NWFP) and (in coalition) in Balochistan, and with its 45 seats in the National Assembly has the power to influence legislation.

An Inconsistent Approach to Islamist Groups

This change in the domestic balance of power has contributed to inconsistencies in the federal government's approach to Islamist groups that advocate violence on grounds of religious difference and oppose Pakistan's participation in the US-led "war on terror". Another factor is the army's reported history of involvement in the nurture and support of Islamist groups. Consequently, the government has vacillated between seeking religious parties' support to counter the secular opposition and cracking down on some of them. Many of the government's policies have not been fully implemented. For example, after suicide attacks in July 2005 in London, UK, the government announced the compulsory registration of all *madrassas*, expulsion of all foreign students by end-2005 and renewed efforts to modernize *madrassas*. None of these measures has been fully enforced. In August 2006, Interior Minister Aftab Ahmed Khan Sherpao confirmed that some 700 foreign *madrassa* students were still in Pakistan and that their visas would be extended to allow them to complete their studies. No decision has been taken about the admission of new students. In February 2006, Prime Minister Shaukat Aziz said that only 9,271 of an estimated 13,000 *madrassas* had been registered. Similarly, no direct action was taken when banned Islamist groups re-emerged under different names or when hate-speech and hate literature continued to contribute to religiously motivated violence.

In its regional relations, the peace process with India, declared "irreversible" by President Musharraf in 2005, has been challenged by domestic Islamic groups who oppose any change in Pakistan's long-standing Kashmir policy. The peace process has recently been shaken by allegations about India's (and Afghanistan's) support for, and funding of, Baloch nationalists, Pakistan's reported discomfort at increasing Indian influence in Afghanistan, and Indian allegations of Pakistani involvement in suicide attacks in Mumbai and elsewhere.

Relations between Pakistan and Afghanistan are encumbered by historical links between sections of the Pakistani leadership, army and intelligence services to fighters against the Soviet Union in Afghanistan. In 2003, Pakistan began a security operation in the designated tribal areas bordering Afghanistan to kill or capture members or associates of al-Qa'ida and the Taleban who fled Afghanistan and their local associates. Currently, some 80,100 army personnel and several hundred platoons of paramilitary forces and tribal police are pursuing foreign fighters fleeing Afghanistan and their Pashtun hosts. After initially focusing on South Waziristan, claimed to be now "almost militant-free" the operation in early 2005 shifted to Bajaur and North Waziristan from where armed clashes continued to be reported until a June 2006 ceasefire was announced by tribal fighters.

The unprecedented control over the tribal areas by the army is by many observers seen to have undermined the status and influence of tribal elders, government-appointed Political Agents and local elected representatives. This leadership vacuum has increasingly been filled by militant clerics, leading to the resurgence of Pashtun groups under the leadership of local clerics, pursuing and enforcing a strict Islamist agenda.

Pakistani Taleban have reportedly enforced strict adherence to their interpretation of Islamic norms of behaviour through their own illegal radio stations and vigilante operations, the dispensation of their own version of "Islamic justice" and targeted killings of government officials and some 150 pro-government tribesmen in the recent past. Many were beheaded and had notes pinned to their bodies warning other collaborators of a similar fate. Some observers have said that "Taleban groups [are] forming shadow governments in the tribal areas". Armed Islamists are reported to be patrolling the streets in towns and villages of the tribal areas, to ensure compliance with their injunctions and Pakistani Taleban have set up checkpoints to collect "taxes" from local traders. Journalists have told Amnesty International that hundreds of tribal families, caught between Taleban threats of cruel punishments and the army's excessive use of force, have fled the tribal areas.

The Taleban Is Strengthening

No effective steps have been taken to stop the Taleban's subversion of the government's authority in the tribal areas. On the contrary, tribal fighters have been strengthened by the increasingly lenient terms offered to them by the government in peace negotiations. In South Waziristan the Shakai Pact of March 2004 stipulated that the tribes cease harbouring foreign fighters and hand them over to the government or ensure their registration. The Pact broke down when one of the signatories of the pact, tribal fighter Nek Mohammad refused to abide by this condition. In the Sararogha Pact of February 2005, the government agreed to pay large sums of money to several tribal fighters to pay off their alleged debts to al-Qa'ida. This pact did not require that foreigners be handed over or registered. The Miramshah Pact of 5 September 2006 provided for the release of arrested tribal fighters, return of their weapons and withdrawal of troops and checkpoints in return for foreigners settled in North Wazirstan respecting the law and renouncing attacks in Afghanistan. Many observers have seen the provision of a safe haven for foreign fighters as a "capitulation" and a "face saving retreat for the Pakistani army" which had suffered considerable losses in the course of the security operation.

Some media reports claim that Pakistani Taleban are joining Afghan Taleban operations, as indicated by several Pakistanis arrested and killed in battles there. Some Pakistani politicians have also accused Pakistan state agencies of supporting the re-emerging Taleban in Afghanistan. Several observers believe that without support from sympathizers in the local ad-

Torture Is Prevalent in Pakistan

The law prohibits torture and other cruel, inhuman, or degrading treatment; there were reports, however, that security forces, including intelligence services, tortured and abused individuals in custody. Under provisions of the Anti-Terrorism Act, coerced confessions are admissible in antiterrorism courts. The NGO [nongovernmental organization] SHARP reported 1,013 cases of torture by police between January and June [2008], including approximately 500 cases by the Punjab police and nearly 350 cases by the Sindh police. Observers noted that underreporting of torture is prevalent in the NWFP [North West Frontier Province] and Balochistan due to local customs. Alleged torture occasionally resulted in death or serious injury.

Human rights organizations reported methods including beating with batons and whips, burning with cigarettes, whipping soles of the feet, prolonged isolation, electric shock, denial of food or sleep, hanging upside down, and forced spreading of the legs with bar fetters.

Security force personnel reportedly raped women during interrogations. The government rarely took action against those responsible. Before the 2006 Women's Protection Act, the Hudood Ordinances allowed Koranic punishments for violations of Shari'a (Islamic law), including amputation and death by stoning. There were no reports that authorities imposed such punishments during the year.

U.S. Department of State,
2008 Human Rights Report: Pakistan,
February 25, 2009.

ministration, Pakistani Taleban could not participate in the fighting nor Afghan fighters withdraw to Pakistan. Others have asked whether the focus on al-Qa'ida members in the context of the "war on terror" to the neglect of Taleban members in the pursuit of the war on terror is related to reported "ambivalence or internal division" in the Pakistani establishment.

Afghan government officials have repeatedly urged Pakistani authorities to stop Taleban infiltration. Similarly, while US officials praise Pakistan as a "key ally" in the "war on terror", they often call for it to take more effective action. Pakistani officials have rejected such criticism saying that Pakistan would take steps on any "actionable material as to where Taleban leaders are", provided by US or NATO [North Atlantic Treaty Organization] forces. In September 2006, President Musharraf admitted that earlier government efforts had focused only on al-Qa'ida members in Pakistani cities and agreed to pursue the Taleban leadership hiding in Pakistan. Pakistani officials have conversely claimed that Afghan authorities had failed to curb Afghan terrorist suspects from infiltrating Pakistan.

US-Pakistani relations have been strained by the growing closeness between the USA and India and the USA's agreement to India's nuclear programme while denying similar recognition to Pakistan. US demands of access to nuclear scientist Dr A.Q. Khan [who is accused of selling nuclear expertise and technology to other countries]; Pakistan's insistence on pursuing a pipeline project with Iran and India despite US objections; Pakistan's traditionally close relations with China; and US foreign policy goals in the Muslim world have further strained bilateral relations.

The Musharraf government will have to find ways to reconcile Pakistan's commitments to pursue the US-led "war on terror" with its duty to protect and promote human rights. It reiterated this commitment when it was elected to the UN [United Nations] Human Rights Council in 2006.

> "The development of a strong and effective education system in Pakistan is central to promoting moderation, tolerance, and economic development."

Education Can End Terrorism in Pakistan

Lisa A. Curtis

In the following viewpoint, Lisa A. Curtis argues that the United States should help reform Pakistan's educational system because doing so will help stabilize Pakistan and make it less likely to fuel terrorism. She maintains that U.S. foreign aid has helped improve the quality of Pakistan's schools, but that the Pakistani government must carry out educational reforms as well. Furthermore, Curtis writes, U.S. policymakers should focus their attention on the small number of madrassas, or Muslim religious schools, that have links to terrorism. The United States should encourage Pakistan to crack down on militant madrassas, while recognizing that most madrassas do not pose a threat. Curtis is a senior research fellow for South Asia in the Asian Studies Center at the Heritage Foundation. The foundation is a conservative think tank.

As you read, consider the following questions:

1. As stated by Curtis, what percentage of Pakistani children complete twelve years of schooling?

2. How do the education programs of the U.S. Agency for International Development empower the local community, as explained by the author?

3. According to Curtis, what should Pakistan do about madrassas that have been linked to terrorism?

A strong and effective education system in Pakistan will help to ensure that the country steers toward a path of stability, moderation, and prosperity in the years to come, and should therefore be a top priority for Washington in its relations with Islamabad [Pakistan's capital]. Lack of adequate education opportunities in Pakistan has contributed to the development of extremist ideologies that have fueled terrorism and sectarian tensions as well as stifled economic growth. Fostering development and reform of the public education system will not only contribute to Pakistani economic prosperity and social tolerance, it will help improve the image of the United States by demonstrating American interest in the human development of average Pakistani citizens.

Today I will focus my remarks on the strengths and weaknesses of current U.S. assistance programs to Pakistan's education sector, as well as the role of the madrassa (Islamic religious school) in contributing to militancy in Pakistan over the last decade.

Pakistan's Schools Have Been Neglected

Pakistan's public education system has suffered from neglect and politicization over the last 30 years. The overall adult literacy rate for the population above the age of 15 is about 43.5 percent, while the rates for Sri Lanka and India are 92 percent and 61 percent, respectively. Female literacy rates in Pakistan are abysmal, standing at about 32 percent. Barely 10 percent of children complete 12 years of schooling. With a population growth rate well over 2 percent, Pakistan is set to add another 100 million people to its current population of 160 million over the next 25 years. About half of this population will be under the age of 18. These demographic trends demand that Pakistan implement significant reforms to its education system and raise literacy rates and skill levels so that these young people can play a productive role in the future economy.

The World Bank and a number of donor agencies spent billions of dollars on a "Social Action Program" for Pakistan during the late 1980s through the 1990s. After a decade, the program failed to achieve basic objectives such as increasing school enrollment rates at the primary level and bringing education to remote parts of the country. The program failed because it did not address problems such as corruption and inefficiency within the Pakistani education bureaucracy. The World Bank's experience should serve as a cautionary tale to the U.S. and other international donors by demonstrating that merely throwing resources at the education sector is unlikely to bring positive results, and that convincing the Pakistani government to reform its own institutions is a necessary part of the process.

The Goals of USAID in Pakistan

U.S. assistance to primary education and literacy in Pakistan has more than doubled—from $28 million in fiscal year 2004 to $66 million in fiscal year 2005. The impact of the findings of the 9/11 Commission report issued in July 2004 on the importance of educational opportunity in the Middle East and South Asia to uprooting terrorist ideology, and increased congressional oversight of U.S. aid programs to Pakistan contributed to the increase in education spending. The Fiscal Year 2008 State Department Congressional Budget Request includes $52 million for general education programs and an additional $50 million for earthquake reconstruction of schools and health facilities. The 2007 Emergency Supplemental Budget Request calls for another $110 million to develop Pakistan's Federally Administered Tribal Areas (FATA), including the education sector. Through a program started in 2003, the United States Agency for International Development (USAID) already is constructing and furnishing 65 primary, middle, and high schools in five agencies of the FATA. The Japanese Government is partnering with the U.S. government on this project and constructing an additional 65 schools in the Tribal Areas.

USAID's education program in Pakistan provides training, technical assistance, and infrastructure for government officials, citizens, and the private sector to deliver high-quality education throughout the country. The program is currently focusing on selected impoverished districts in the Sindh and Baluchistan provinces in addition to the FATA (see above). The Basic Education Program benefits over 367,000 Pakistani children and USAID has so far trained over 16,000 Pakistani teachers and administrators. USAID also provides funding for needs-based scholarships for higher education and grants for Fulbright scholarships for post-graduate degrees in the U.S.

USAID education programs also focus on empowering the local community by fostering partnerships between parents and teachers that improve accountability for the children's education. I had the opportunity to visit a USAID-funded girls' school on the outskirts of Islamabad in late 2005. Through a grant of only $1,500, USAID inspired the people of this community to establish a Parent-Teacher Association and to build a library for the school that serves over 500 students.

While this kind of outreach at the grassroots level is necessary, Washington also needs to encourage the Pakistani government to follow through on its own reforms. The government of President Pervez Musharraf launched its Education Sector Reforms (ESR) in January 2002, but has been unwilling to commit substantial resources to reforming the education sector. For example, the government has yet to follow through on its commitment to raise the education budget to four percent of GDP [gross domestic product] in line with United Nations Educational, Scientific, and Cultural Organization recommendations.

One of the major problems with Pakistan's public education sector has been the endemic corruption within the system, which has led to the phenomenon of "ghost schools," i.e. teachers not showing up to teach classes but only to collect their paychecks. The U.S. can help by supporting teacher training programs and encouraging greater accountability through community involvement, but the Pakistani government will have to do its part to limit corruption and inefficiency within the system.

The U.S. Needs to Pay Attention to Certain Madrassas

The role of the madrassa in Pakistan and its contribution to Islamic militancy has been the subject of intense debate in U.S. academic and policy circles. Observers have been unable to agree on the actual numbers of madrassas and madrassa students in Pakistan, and some studies reveal that the international media has exaggerated these figures during the last few years. A World Bank study from 2005, for example, says Pakistani madrassas account for less than 1 percent of total academic enrollment in the country. In April 2002, Dr. Mahmood Ahmed Ghazi, the former Pakistani Minister of Religious Affairs, put the number of madrassas at about 10,000, with 1.7 million students.

While most madrassas in Pakistan are not churning out terrorist foot soldiers, there are a handful of religious seminaries that promote anti-West, pan-Islamic, and violent ideologies. Many of the older madrassas have well-established reputations for producing serious Islamic thinkers, while oth-

Economic Progress Can Also Prevent Terrorism

[Terrorist groups] recruit disaffected youth in significant numbers who are willing to commit suicide to destroy enemies. Just as economic progress greatly affects family structure and the amount of freedom available, it also sharply reduces the willingness of people to hide or otherwise protect terrorists because they have more to lose if they are caught. Although leaders of terrorist organizations usually come from more educated classes, these organizations rely on numerous foot soldiers to do a lot of the dirty work. They are generally recruited from younger and less educated groups. It becomes much harder to recruit many of these soldiers when good jobs are available.

Gary Becker,
"Does Economic Development Reduce Terrorism?"
The Becker-Pusher Blog, January 6, 2008.

ers provide welfare services to the poor through free religious education, lodging, and food. A madrassa student learns how to read, memorize, and recite the Quran, and those with advanced theological training become Ulema (religious scholars). Each of the different schools of Islamic thought in Pakistan, including the Sunni Deobandis, Barelvis, Ahle-Hadith (Salafi), and Jamaat-e-Islami (JI) as well as the Shiia, runs its own seminaries.

From a counterterrorism perspective, U.S. policymakers should focus their attention on the handful of madrassas in Pakistan that have well-established links to terrorism. These madrassas are likely well known to the Pakistani authorities and increasingly to U.S. intelligence and policy officials, and deserve special focus in our counterterrorism policies. The Darul Uloom Haqqania located near Peshawar in the Northwest Frontier Province, for example, served as training ground for Taliban leaders and a recruiting center for Pakistani militants fighting in Kashmir.

Other madrassas connected to violent militancy are located in the southern port city of Karachi as well as in the province of Punjab and have also contributed to sectarian tensions in the country. The banned Kashmiri militant organization Jaish-e-Muhammad (JEM, or "Army of the Prophet") and Sunni sectarian organization Sepah-e-Sahaba (SSP, or "Army of Companions of the Prophet") are headquartered in southern Punjab. These organizations have close institutional links with the Taliban and have been involved in terrorism against Indian and Western targets, including the murder of *Wall Street Journal* reporter Daniel Pearl in 2002; the hijacking of an Indian Airlines flight that landed in Kandahar, Afghanistan, in December 1999; and the kidnapping and murder of five Western hostages, including American citizen Donald Hutchings, in 1995.

These madrassas and associated militant groups have an interdependent relationship in which the militant groups provide armed backing for the madrassas, and the madrassas in turn provide motivated recruits for the militant organizations. The recently jailed leader of a fertilizer bomb plot in England—British citizen of Pakistani-origin Omar Khyam—was reportedly inspired and trained by Pakistanis involved in militancy in Kashmir. In addition, one of the suicide bombers who carried out the July 7, 2005, bombings of the London transport system reportedly spent time at a Pakistani madrassa. Convincing the Pakistan government to completely close down these dangerous militant groups and to sever their links with the madrassas should be the centerpiece of our counterterrorism policies in Pakistan.

Government Reform of Madrassas Has Been Unsuccessful

Madrassas in Pakistan are financed either by voluntary charity, foreign entities, or governments. The Saudi Arabian organization, Harmain Islamic Foundation, reportedly has provided substantial financial assistance to the Ahle-Hadith madrassas, which have provided fighters to the banned Kashmiri militant group Lashkar-e-Tayyaba (LET). The Ahle-Hadith madrassas emphasize the Quran and Hadith (sayings of the Prophet Muhammed) and oppose folk Islam and practices such as celebrating the anniversaries of saints or the distribution of food on religious occasions. The large madrassa complex supporting LET is located in the town of Muridke outside of Lahore and is well known for preaching hard-line views on Islam. Since the Pakistan government officially banned LET in 2002, the group has changed its name to Jamaat-ul-Dawa and played a significant role in assisting victims following the October 8, 2005, South Asia earthquake, demonstrating its ability to operate freely within Pakistani society.

President Musharraf's government has had little success with its attempts to assert greater government authority over the madrassas. In August of 2001, the Musharraf government promulgated the "Pakistan Madrassa Education Board Ordinance 2001" to establish three model madrassa institutions in Karachi, Sukkur, and Islamabad that would include English, math, computer science, economics, political science, law, and Pakistan studies in their curricula. Through the "Voluntary Registration and Regulation Ordinance 2002," the government promised funding to madrassas that formally registered with the government. In a more controversial step, the Pakistani government demanded that madrassas expel all foreign students by December 31, 2005. Islamist groups vehemently resisted the government's efforts, however, and authorities backed down and made public statements indicating that they would not use force or shut down noncompliant madrassas to enforce the directives.

The Minister for Religious Affairs, Ejaz ul-Haq, son of the late former President Zia ul-Haq, is responsible for implementing madrassa reform. It was Zia ul-Haq's Islamization policies in the 1980s that resulted in an expansion of the madrassa network to support the Afghanistan jihad ["holy war"] against the Soviets and that incorporated militant interpretations of Islam into the public school curriculum. Minister Ejaz ul-Haq has so far been reluctant to confront the prominent religious parties that have ties to foreign-funded madrassas and are resisting government reform.

Recommendations for U.S. Policy

The U.S. should begin to program more funds for specific education and development projects rather than continue to provide the bulk of our economic assistance in the form of a direct cash transfer to the Pakistani government. Since 2004, the U.S. has provided $200 million annually to Pakistan in the form of direct budgetary support. We have established a consulting mechanism with the Pakistan government to try to ensure a portion of this money is spent on the health and education sectors. However, we cannot fully ensure that this U.S. taxpayer money is contributing to economic and human development in Pakistan. The U.S. also reaps very little public diplomacy benefits with the broader Pakistani population from this large amount of aid, which most Pakistanis view as mainly benefiting the Musharraf regime. Congress should require that at least two-thirds of our total economic support fund assistance be in the form of USAID project assistance related to education, health, and economic and democratic development.

While continuing to help train teachers and increase the quality of education in Pakistani schools, Washington also will need to encourage Islamabad to implement systemic reform of public education in order to make a significant impact on education outcomes, such as increased literacy and enrollment rates and decreased dropout rates. U.S. policymakers and aid officials need to take to heart the results of the failed World Bank efforts from the 1980s through the 1990s to avoid repeating similar mistakes. Pushing for systemic reform may require the U.S. to increasingly use benchmarks with the Pakistani government in order to encourage greater efficiency and transparency within the education bureaucracy.

Washington will need to encourage Pakistan to crack down on those madrassas that continue to promote extremist violence and sectarian policies that lead to terrorism and the destabilization of Pakistani society. The Pakistani authorities should clean house in any madrassas found to have links to international terrorist incidents and make clear that those individuals who provide protection or safe haven to al-Qaeda and like-minded terrorist groups will be held to account. The Pakistan government's refusal to detain or punish key terrorist leaders because of their links to the Kashmir militancy signals a degree of tolerance of terrorist activity and provides a permissible environment for groups that collaborate with al-Qaeda and other terrorist groups. The Pakistan authorities likely know which madrassas are supplying militants for terrorist training. We should use skillful diplomacy to persuade the Pakistani government to reform or close down these schools.

The U.S. should refrain from getting involved in Pakistan's broader madrassa reform efforts and accept that many of the traditional madrassas serve a useful purpose in educating Islamic intellectuals and providing shelter and food for impoverished youth. While a few Pakistani madrassas represent an international terrorist threat and deserve American scrutiny and condemnation, most madrassas should be left alone.

To conclude, U.S. efforts to encourage education reform and development in Pakistan should be consistent, sustained, and multi-pronged. Ensuring transparency and efficiency in the education bureaucracy is equally important to encouraging local community involvement and accountability in the day-to-day functioning of individual schools, especially in poor, rural areas. The development of a strong and effective education system in Pakistan is central to promoting moderation, tolerance, and economic development. Convincing the Pakistani government to take firm action against the handful of madrassas supporting violent extremism also is necessary, not only for the future stability of Pakistan, but also to prevent future international terrorism.

Periodical Bibliography

Aryn Baker   "The Central Front," *Time*, September 11, 2008.

Don Belt   "Struggle for the Soul of Pakistan," *National Geographic*, September 2007.

Economist   "Taliban All Over," April 14, 2007.

Economist   "United Against the Wrong Enemy," December 20, 2008.

Reuel Marc Gerecht   "Our Pakistan Problem," *Weekly Standard*, December 22, 2008.

Thomas K. Grose   "Why Britain Increasingly Worries About Pakistani Terrorism," *U.S. News & World Report*, December 24, 2008.

Adnan R. Khan   "Danger Zone," *Maclean's*, February 25, 2008.

Aamir Latif   "After Suicide Bombing, Can Pakistan Launch a Credible Offensive Against Terrorism?" *U.S. News & World Report*, September 22, 2008.

Anna Mulrine   "Bad Guys in the Border Lands," *U.S. News & World Report*, June 23, 2008.

Fraser Nelson   "Don't Mention the Afghan-Pakistan War," *Spectator*, July 26, 2008.

Thomas Omestad   "Why the Obama Administration Is So Worried About Pakistan," *U.S. News & World Report*, April 28, 2009.

David Pilling   "The Question Is: Which Is the Real Pakistan?" *Financial Times*, February 12, 2009.

CHAPTER 3

What Should the U.S. Role Be in Pakistan?

Chapter Preface

The role of the United States in helping Pakistan become more politically stable and improve its citizens' quality of life does not fall solely under the purview of the U.S. government. One man, American Greg Mortenson, has helped improve the quality of education in Pakistan by creating a movement to build schools throughout the nation.

Pakistan's educational system is severely underfunded. While the United Nations recommends that developing economies spend 4 percent of their gross domestic product on education, Pakistan budgets only 2.4 percent. Not surprisingly, this translates into a 55 percent adult literacy rate. Among young adults (ages fifteen to twenty-four years old), the literacy rate is 80 percent for males and 60 percent for females. With 60 percent of the nation's population under the age of eighteen, it becomes imperative for Pakistan to build its educational infrastructure, because poor and uneducated Pakistanis are more likely to be recruited by the Taliban.

Greg Mortenson's effort to fund and build schools, as detailed in his memoir *Three Cups of Tea*, has helped thousands of Pakistanis. Mortenson first came to Pakistan in 1993 with the aim of climbing the mountain K2. Following that climb, he became aware of the lack of schools in remote areas of Pakistan and Afghanistan and pledged to help those nations. Since that time he has helped fund and build 90 schools that have educated more than 34,000 children, with an emphasis placed on educating girls. He is helped in his efforts by the Central Asia Institute.

Mortenson's work has been widely praised because it shows how Americans and others in the international community can improve life in Pakistan and bring about a more peaceful future. *New York Times* columnist, Nicholas D. Kristoff opines, "I have this fantasy: Suppose that the United States focused

... more on working through local aid groups to build schools, simultaneously cutting tariffs on Pakistani and Afghan manufactured exports. There would be no immediate payback, but a better-educated and more economically vibrant Pakistan would probably be more resistant to extremism." It could take many years for such an effort to meet its goals, but the success of Mortenson and his supporters suggest that a variety of U.S. aid can improve life in Pakistan. The authors in this chapter evaluate the role of the United States in Pakistan.

| *"[Pakistan] will need U.S. assistance and support to provide economic development and strengthen democracy."*

The United States Must Help Pakistan Achieve Democracy

Hassan Abbas

In the following viewpoint, Hassan Abbas contends that Pakistan has a variety of economic and political problems that cannot be addressed without aid and support from the United States. Among the issues that Pakistan can tackle with the help of the United States are the rise of Islamic extremism, as well as incompetent government policies and inadequate schools that have failed to improve the lives of average Pakistanis. According to Abbas, support for Pakistan will strengthen U.S. interests in the Middle East. Abbas is an author and a former member of the Pakistani government.

As you read, consider the following questions:

1. According to Abbas, what single factor is behind Muslim hatred for U.S. policies?

2. In the author's view, what did Pakistan choose over building hospitals and schools?

3. How would Abbas solve the conflict between Pakistan and India over Kashmir?

America has often wondered aloud why many Muslims did not strongly condemn the outrageous terrorist attacks on 9/11. While the reasons behind the Muslim masses' seeming lack of condemnation are complex and varied, one of the more direct and honest answers to this is that a large percentage of Muslims all around the world perceive America itself as, if not the perpetrator, then at least as the instigator of similar outrages and injustices. Others wondered aloud: "Why do they hate us?" and this anguish is heard around the world. But for years before this, many in Muslim countries have been asking: "What compels America to be so unjust?" Except for some intellectuals, journalists, and academics, none in the United States had taken this plaintive cry seriously.

For decades, higher national interests have compelled successive American administrations to support highly repressive regimes in many Muslim countries. A clean example is that of Saddam Hussein, who was a close enough ally to be equipped with weapons by Western countries, including the United States, during the eight-year war that he fought against Iran. After the war, he used these weapons against his own Kurdish and Shia populations. The irony is that, in this age of rapid communications, the average American heard about the plight of these Kurds and Shias only a good ten (or, in some cases, fifteen) years after the gruesome event. Neither did this average American hear about what the secret police of the Shah of Iran, or that of the house of Saud or of the Egyptian dictators do to their own people. These people suffered an unbroken tyranny spanning many decades. Helpless and powerless, they could only hate their leaders. By extension, they hated America, the main prop of these regimes that had treated them inhumanely. Further, no single factor has stoked the fires of hate in Muslim countries as have the U.S. policies affecting Israel and the Palestinians. These were always seen as being tilted in favor of Israel.

But this question of "hate," when posed by the average American, who is the least xenophobic [fearful of foreigners] among the peoples of the world, remains germane [relevant]. Because he harbors no resentment against the peoples of distant countries, the extraordinary lengths that the latter will go for the sole purpose of harming him can only bewilder him. He cannot realize that the illiterate Muslim fanatic is least qualified to tell the difference between some of the U.S. government policies and the American people. Therefore, this spiral of hate, built on real or perceived injustice, got further entrenched with the passage of time.

Changing Views Toward America

Pakistan, not being an Arab country and being far from the scene of conflict in the Israel-Palestine region, could have been expected not to harbor anti-American feelings of the strain and virulence of those harbored by many Arabs. That indeed was the case in the early days of Pakistan, and the reasons for this were that Pakistan was a very early ally of America, receiving substantial military and economic aid; the focus of Pakistani animus [ill will] and suspicions was pointed toward India; the religious parties had good working relations with the United States; and last but not least, the Pakistani military regimes supported by the United States were not as harsh and brutal as those in the Middle East. Because of the combined effect of all these factors, far from being anti-American, the general public sentiment was very much pro-U.S., and this continued to be the case until the mid-1960s.

After the 1965 [India–Pakistan] war there was the first, though muted, burst of anti-Americanism experienced in Pakistan because the United States (despite being an ally) did not come to Pakistan's assistance. This mood did not last. It was after the 1967 Arab-Israeli war that anti-Israeli emotion took root in Pakistan, which eventually extended to the United States as well. Profiting from this opportunity, religious parties declared Jews and Israel the root of much of the malevolence afflicting Muslims all over the world and, by extension, Pakistan. But this newfound scapegoat did not take immediate hold.

The next crucial stage in this context was the Palestinian Intifada, which Pakistanis witnessed through the television screen. They repeatedly saw Israeli attacks on the West Bank and Gaza with the U.S.-made helicopters and tanks while Palestinian youth were shown opposing these attacks with slings and stones. The stark inequality of the contest left an imprint on their minds and thus the issue was constantly discussed. Hence, the religious parties on their recruitment drives needed nothing more. Religious leaders were to cash in on these passions to gain personal popularity, and then turn them into anti-American rage in coming years. The American betrayal in Afghanistan in 1989–1990 was to only add fuel to the fire of anti-Americanism in Pakistan.

Resulting from a lack of educational opportunities, an ongoing sense of strategic insecurity, and streams of financial support from Wahhabi sources in the Arab states, the *Madrasa* [religious school] industry had also caught on in Pakistan in the aftermath of the Afghan war of the 1980s, and the assembly line was producing tens of thousands of deadly earnest future "heroes." Their one unity is their common hatred of the westernized Pakistani elite, India, America, and Israel. Because of India, their focus and attention on America is divided, but their commitment to give their lives for what they believe in, irrespective of who is on the other side, is not expected to diminish. And though Pakistani generals and politicians are still given to making their habitual noises, the very tepidness of their calls to end the power of religious extremist groups is like the fading strains of a distant retreat; the much vaunted power of the army is increasingly a façade that must crack sooner or later, and the power that is on the ascendant is that of the religious parties.

It was hoped that the anti-Osama [bin Laden] operation would stabilize and strengthen Pakistan. It was hoped that the United States would start its reconstruction of Afghanistan through Pakistan—to strengthen first its base, and then move into the area of instability and uncertainty. Unfortunately, this did not happen. The little aid that Pakistan received was more than counterbalanced by the expenses involved in keeping its forces deployed on the borders in response to the Indian threat in 2002–3. Thus, no economic activity came to relieve Pakistan's stagnation. The *Madrasa* remains the only haven for the child whose parents can not afford him. Pakistan's alliance with the United States in the aftermath of the U.S. campaign in Afghanistan yet again brought no tangible benefit to the people of Pakistan.

The Tragedy of Pakistan

Criminal incompetence in governance and lack of funds for the public education system further strained Pakistan's capacity to change for the better. The real tragedy is that a country that has produced a Nobel Prize-winner in physics and so many top-class physicians, high-tech geniuses, and some of the finest air force pilots in the world has wasted so much due to the inadequacy of its education system for the masses, robbing so many of a chance to succeed in life. Pakistan preferred acquiring F-16s and submarines over establishing schools and hospitals. Billions of dollars spent on defense procurements provided security only to the military, political, and bureaucratic elite of Pakistan. For ordinary people these policies brought hunger, misery, and hopelessness.

Failing to make a real difference lately, [President Pervez] Musharraf has fallen in the esteem of the people of Pakistan, and there is many a hope that lies crushed in the rubble of this fall, and yet no popular movement has been able to generate steam against him. That, however, is only a matter of time, and unfortunately the ones who will lead the public opinion in such a crisis will be the religious leaders, because Musharraf has sidelined the liberal forces and moderate political parties. Without doubt, Musharraf has shown ample courage in fighting religious extremism and terrorism, but has failed to institutionalize his policies. A credible democratic set-up could have strengthened Musharraf, but he opted to sponsor the "King's Party," which will be history the day Musharraf leaves the scene.

Barring a miracle, the influence of the rightist parties is bound to grow in Pakistan, or at the very least they will retain a solid following. The U.S. attack on Iraq is viewed in Pakistan as a step in the establishment of a new imperialism. Indeed, this war has pulled the rug out from under the feet of the Pakistani moderates and given the clerics new strength. Even before the Iraq war started in early 2003, the U.S. campaign in Afghanistan, leading to thousands of civilian deaths, and the U.S. ultimatums to Iraq were enough to convince them about what was ahead, and that gave them sufficient support to demonstrate their power in the October 2002 general elections, in which they had their best showing ever in terms of winning seats in the central and provincial legislatures. Yet it is unlikely that they will come to power in the future through the ballot. It is more likely that an errant spark somewhere will ignite massive street protests, and if these protests are joined by the jihadi ["holy war"] groups and the army is called out to contain them, it will be a real disaster for Pakistan.

The Pakistan Army dare not confront them, knowing their strength and suspecting that they have many sympathizers, if not supporters, within its own ranks. It was therefore considered more feasible for the army to continue to direct its energies in the battle zone of Kashmir rather than to face the jiha-dis. It was for the convenience of its repose that the army, routinely given to having study periods on a myriad of sub-jects, has apparently not done one on the strength and poten-tial of the jihadi organizations. No one has a clear idea about their exact numbers, but their potential capability resides in the subconscious of those in authority, and this stays there be-cause the reality of it is too hard to confront. Their funding will not dry up because thousands of Pakistanis and Arabs be-lieve in them and contribute to them.

Pakistan Must Reduce the Power of Extremists

To tackle this, Pakistan must devise ways to lessen the power and influence of religious extremists in the country and sup-port genuine Islamic scholarship as a counter. Most of Islam is very simple to understand and therefore needs little inter-pretation. Mullah [a religious master] scholarship, as it has turned out to be, moves from the broad to the narrow, em-phasizing the arcane over the easily intelligible. By its very na-ture, therefore, it must reside in narrow crevices and attempt to broaden them into irreconcilable differences. It is in finding and defining such differences that mullah scholarship, as dis-tinct from that of the Sufi (mystic) or a true *alim* (scholar), gains approval of the multitude, who gasp with wonder as they are initiated into the intricate world of hairsplitting. The narrow intellectualism of the mullah can only be divisive, ex-clusive, and intolerant of those whom it excludes, and is anti-thetical to all that is eclectic and harmonizing.

If Pakistan is to be saved from its likely future, it must in-vest in its envisioned future, and start doing so now. It must start by coming to a sincere accommodation with India over Kashmir. To make this possible, India too will have to shed its present position on Kashmir and proffer an equally sincere hand of friendship to Pakistan. Perhaps India should initially

American Support Has Not Been Helpful

A succession of administrations in Washington have backed a series of wrong horses in [Pakistani capital] Islamabad: military dictators like [Pervez] Musharraf or feudal aristocrats like [Benazir] Bhutto. "We have a bad habit of always personalizing our foreign policy," says P.J. Crowley, senior fellow at the Center for American Progress. Little effort has ever been made to look past individuals and encourage or engage with the institutions of Pakistan civil society. The most recent example of this neglect came last summer [2007] when Pakistani lawyers and judges protested Musharraf's summary sacking of an independent-minded Supreme Court judge; they received little more than lip service from Washington, which was more concerned about Musharraf's survival.

Nor has the cause of Pakistani democracy been helped by the U.S. habit of giving more money to Pakistan's military leaders than to its civilian ones. Husain Haqqani, a former diplomat and political confidant of Benazir Bhutto's, told Congress last October that since 1954 the U.S. has given Pakistan about $21 billion in aid, of which $17. 7 billion was given under military rule, and only $3.4 billion to elected governments.

Simon Robinson,
"Why Pakistan Matters,"
Time, *January 14, 2008.*

enlarge the autonomy in Kashmir, to which Pakistan could respond by creating further space and circumstances for India. In a second stage, India and Pakistan could work out the modalities of a jointly controlled Kashmir Valley, turning the bone of contention into a peace bridge between the two countries. And concurrently with this, Pakistan should take every measure to effect an economic upturn conspicuous enough to give its people real hope.

And all this is impossible to achieve in the absence of strong democratic institutions. Democracy is not alien to Pakistan. It had come into being as a democracy, though autocratic tendencies of the Pakistani elite and military dictators changed its direction. Still, the people of Pakistan yearn for true democracy. For this dream to become a reality, Pakistan's military establishment has to take a back seat.

Pakistan will not be able to do this on its own. It will need U.S. assistance and support to provide economic development and strengthen democracy. At a global level it may be worth America's while to invest in peace, a small price to pay compared to the cost of war. Funds and support must be carefully allocated and invested so as to avoid both a repeat cycle of corruption and an unending rentier-state status [a state reliant on externally generated revenues, or rents (in Pakistan's case, external sources are in the form of foreign aid and loans)] for Pakistan. The new confidence that unchallenged power has given to the United States has made it prone to unilateralism and to see war as a solution to problems. Sooner or later it must realize that it cannot bomb an idea out of existence. The answer lies in positing another and more powerful idea. If injustice has sparked a fire, it will be justice that will douse it— not more injustice. If there has to be universal peace, it shall be born not out of the "infinite," but out of universal justice. It is certainly within the United States' means and interests to help usher in such an era.

> "Against all logic, the United States has
> treated Pakistan as an indispensable
> ally, . . . while ignoring Pakistan's
> checkered history of heedless nuclear
> proliferation."

The United States Should Not Support Pakistan

Charles Scaliger

The United States should not provide foreign aid to Pakistan because doing so helps strengthen Pakistan's nuclear capability, Charles Scaliger argues in the following viewpoint. According to Scaliger, Pakistan's nuclear program is a serious concern because the nation is run by a military dictatorship that sells blueprints for building nuclear weapons to Iran and China; more troubling, writes Scaliger, is that Islamic extremists could come to power and gain control of these weapons. Furthermore, Scaliger contends, the United States is culpable in the development of Pakistan's nuclear program because of espionage by a U.S. State Department official. Scaliger is a teacher and writer.

Charles Scaliger, "Parting with Pakistan: Our 'Valuable Ally'," *The New American*, vol. 24, February 4, 2008. Copyright © 2008 American Opinion Publishing Incorporated. Reproduced by permission.

As you read, consider the following questions:

1. How many warheads are in Pakistan's nuclear arsenal, according to Scaliger?

2. As stated by the author, which nuclear scientist sold nuclear weapons designs to Iran, Libya, and North Korea?

3. In Scaliger's view, what examples of meddling in the Middle East have not benefited the United States?

Whatever Pakistan's founder Muhammed Ali-Jinnah may have envisioned for the future of his country, it certainly was not this. A proverbial land of contrasts, Pakistan boasts some of the world's loftiest mountains as well as vast stretches of hot, parched desert; teeming cities as well as sparsely populated frontier regions where the forces of law and order seldom venture; a government organized along British constitutional lines but enshrining Islam as the state religion; and a remnant of forward-thinking, Western-leaning intellectual and political elites hard pressed by widespread Islamic radicalism. The recent [December 2007] assassination of Pakistan's grande dame, Benazir Bhutto, has focused the attention of the world on the desperate plight of the world's second-largest Muslim state (after Indonesia), but the deepening crisis there transcends the current partisan violence.

Pakistan Has a Troubled History

What is surprising about modern-day Pakistan is not that the country is lurching toward collapse and civil war, but that it has taken so long to happen. For Pakistan was birthed in blood, and her history since 1947, the year of her founding, has featured four major wars, numerous military incidents with archrival India, and a government that has oscillated between popularly elected prime ministers and military dictatorship.

Originally part of the Raj, or British India, the territory that became Pakistan (including modern-day Bangladesh, formerly East Pakistan) was the subject of a bitter tug of war between India's Congress Party, led by the likes of Mahatma Gandhi and Jawaharlal Nehru, and the Muslim League, led by the intractable Jinnah. It was Gandhi's hope that India after independence would remain a single country and that Muslim and Hindu would be able to set aside religious differences in the interest of national unity. But it was not to be. The so-called Partition of India at independence brought about one of the largest migrations in human history, with millions of Hindus leaving Pakistani territory to settle in India, and millions of Muslims departing India for what at the time were deemed the greener pastures of the "Land of the Pure."

Yet subsequent history has decided the issue in favor of Gandhi's vision. India, itself home to a Muslim population only slightly smaller than Pakistan's, has made steady progress, especially during the last decade and a half or so, and is rapidly being transformed into another Asian economic success story. While religious tensions have occasionally flared into full-blown bloodletting, India has held together and managed to sustain, with the exception of a single notorious interlude of dictatorship (Indira Gandhi's "Emergency"), an elected, secular government, religious freedom, and a robust free press—this in a neighborhood also featuring the likes of Communist China and Burma.

Pakistan, by contrast, remains one of the poorest countries in Asia, with little or no economic growth to be shown for decades of misrule. Brutal military dictatorships have generally been the remedy for corrupt popular government; the latest, Pervez Musharraf's corruption-ridden autocracy, has run roughshod over Pakistan's constitution for nearly a decade and enriched Pakistan's military at the expense of everybody else.

Pakistan's Nuclear Program Is a Major Concern

When Pakistan embarked on an ambitious nuclear program in the 1970s, then-Prime Minister Zulfikar Ali Bhutto (father of Benazir) famously and callously remarked that, rather than let India monopolize nuclear weapons in South Asia, his people would even "eat grass" if the transfer of resources to the nuclear program demanded it.

And so the people have, almost literally. By current estimates, Pakistan has a nuclear arsenal of around 100 warheads, developed after decades of expensive research, nuclear espionage, and the construction of multiple enrichment facilities. Her military bristles with an impressive array of state-of the-art strategic missiles and other modern weapons. Yet her economy is still largely agricultural, and most of her 160 million inhabitants endure a standard of living of which Medieval European serfs would scarcely be envious.

It is Pakistan's nuclear program, against a combustible backdrop of turbulent Pakistani politics and international terrorism, that is of paramount geopolitical concern. Pakistan's nuclear arsenal, so far, is designed for regional, not global, strategic parity, and, unlike China or Russia, Pakistan has neither the means nor, apparently, the inclination to square off against the United States.

But Pakistan, like India and Israel, is not a signatory to the Nuclear Non-proliferation Treaty. Unlike the other two, Pakistan has been a flagrant exporter of nuclear technology. From the mid-seventies onward, Pakistan has been the world's major trafficker in nuclear secrets, stealing technology from the United States and Western European countries and selling the information to the highest bidder. Revered Pakistani nuclear scientist Abdul Qadeer Khan ran an international nuclear black market for decades. It was Khan, mastermind of the 1998 Pakistani nuclear tests, who sold nuclear weapons designs and other information to North Korea, Iran, and Libya,

The U.S. Should Look at the Influence of Other Nations on Pakistan

U.S. policymakers should be asking who else is giving support to Pakistan and what influence their money is having. Given Islamabad's [Pakistan's capital] displeasure with the recent U.S.-Indian nuclear deal and its consideration of Beijing [China] as an "all-weather friend," U.S. officials ought to look more closely at the full nature of China's military and economic support to Pakistan. Washington should also investigate how much money is being channeled to Pakistan from the Persian Gulf through Islamic charities and for what purposes. This is broader than merely disturbing terrorist financing; it goes to the heart of the battle of ideas being waged.

Craig Cohen and Derek Chollet,
Washington Quarterly, *Spring 2007.*

greatly increasing the likelihood that such weapons might ultimately fall into the hands of terrorists. Most ominously of all, scant weeks before 9/11, Khan's aides are believed to have met with Osama bin Laden to discuss nuclear weapons for al-Qaeda.

Pakistan's current military dictator, Pervez Musharraf, reacting to U.S. pressure, eventually placed Khan under house arrest and reluctantly cooperated with the United States in shutting down the Pakistani nuclear bazaar. But after Khan performed the appropriate lustrations—confessing to having supplied North Korea and other terrorist states with nuclear technology on national television—he was pardoned by President Musharraf.

The United States Is Aiding Pakistan's Dictatorship

Despite such activities, President [George W.] Bush failed to mention Pakistan in his famous "Axis of Evil" speech. This is because, against all logic, the United States has treated Pakistan as an indispensable ally, doling out generous amounts of foreign aid while ignoring Pakistan's checkered history of heedless nuclear proliferation. American largess, to a military dictator armed with nuclear weapons, obviously has done nothing to ameliorate the situation. Instead, our support for Musharraf has strengthened his hand.

Now there's a new wrinkle. A January 6 [2008] *London Times* article alleges that high-ranking officials at the Pentagon and U.S. State Department helped to supply Turkish intermediaries with classified American nuclear technology that was then sold to Pakistani agents, according to the explosive testimony of former FBI [U.S. Federal Bureau of Investigation] translator Sibel Edmonds. Edmonds, who is fluent in both Turkish and Farsi, claims she was privy to evidence-gathering on certain U.S. officials, who are "household names," selling nuclear technology to Turkish and Israeli agents. "If you made public all the information that the FBI have on this case, you will see very high-level people going through criminal trials," Edmonds was quoted as saying. According to the *Times* story, which has been ignored by the major media in the United States:

> The Turks and Israelis had planted "moles" in military and academic institutions which handled nuclear technology. Edmonds says there were several transactions of nuclear material every month, with the Pakistanis being among the eventual buyers. "The network appeared to be obtaining information from every nuclear agency in the United States," she said.
>
> They were helped, she says, by the high-ranking State Department official who provided some of their moles—mainly

PhD students—with security clearance to work in sensitive nuclear research facilities. These included the Los Alamos nuclear laboratory in New Mexico, which is responsible for the security of the US nuclear deterrent.

In one conversation Edmonds heard the official arranging to pick up a $15,000 cash bribe. The package was to be dropped off at an agreed location by someone in the Turkish diplomatic community who was working for the network.

The Turks, she says, often acted as a conduit for the Inter-Services Intelligence (ISI), Pakistan's spy agency, because they were less likely to attract suspicion. Venues such as the American Turkish Council in Washington were used to drop off the cash, which was picked up by the official. . . .

The Pakistani operation was led by General Mahmoud Ahmad, then the ISI chief.

Intercepted communications showed Ahmad and his colleagues stationed in Washington were in constant contact with attaches in the Turkish embassy.

That is, according to Edmonds, the Pakistani dictatorship is the beneficiary of U.S. foreign aid, and its nuclear program has directly benefited from espionage facilitated by a high-ranking U.S. State Department official. The *Times* article continues: "Intelligence analysts say that members of the ISI were close to Al-Qaeda before and after 9/11. Indeed, Ahmad was accused of sanctioning a $100,000 wire payment to Mohammed Atta, one of the 9/11 hijackers, immediately before the attacks."

The U.S. Should Stop Sending Aid to Pakistan

This, then, is the Pakistan from which a succession of U.S. presidents—George W. Bush is only the latest—have refused to disengage, a hotbed of Islamic radicalism and probable safe haven for Osama bin Laden, Ayman al-Zawahiri, and other al-Qaeda operatives, and a fickle military dictatorship that does not scruple to sell blueprints for the world's deadliest weapons to Tehran [Iran] and Pyongyang [North Korea].

What should the United States do about the escalating Pakistani crisis? At the very least, cease and desist from sending foreign aid to Islamabad [Pakistan's capital]. It is too late to put Pakistan's nuclear genie back into the bottle, but it is not too late to avoid further inflaming tensions in the region by meddling where we ought not. Other meddling in the Mideast, such as the U.S. government's support of Saddam Hussein prior to the Persian Gulf War, or our support of Osama bin Laden during the Soviet occupation of Afghanistan, has not benefited our country or ended Middle East tensions. And neither has our aid to Musharraf.

Although Pakistan is not a declared enemy of the United States like Iran or North Korea, continuing to accommodate Pakistani dictators and ignoring Pakistan's irresponsible nuclear proliferation may hasten the day when Islamic extremists come to power there—and gain access to the world's most dangerous weapons.

| "I have long believed that we need to use our economic assistance to build a long term relationship with Pakistan."

The United States Must Work to Improve Pakistan's Economic and Political Situation

Teresita C. Schaffer

In the following viewpoint, Teresita C. Schaffer argues that Pakistan is undergoing a variety of domestic and national security problems that the United States can help solve through political, military, and economic aid. She contends that providing economic and military assistance is a way to build a long-term relationship with Pakistan and help that nation invest in the education and health of its citizens. Support for free and fair elections is also vital if Pakistan is to quell the rise of violent extremists. Schaffer is the director of the South Asia program at the Center for Strategic and International Studies, a bipartisan organization that researches and develops policy initiatives on global issues.

Teresita C. Schaffer, testimony before Senate Foreign Relations Committee, Subcommittee on the Near East and South Asia, July 25, 2007.

As you read, consider the following questions:

1. According to Schaffer, what is the first drama playing out in Pakistan?

2. Why does the author oppose U.S. military intervention in Pakistan's tribal areas?

3. What is Schaffer's final recommendation?

M r. Chairman, members of the Committee, thank you for inviting me to appear before you. Pakistan today [2007] is going through the most severe crisis it has faced in the past eight years. Its future matters profoundly to the United States and to the region, so it is a good time to take stock of U.S. policy.

I would like to sketch out briefly the multiple crises Pakistan now faces. I conclude that the United States needs to put its weight behind a return to civilian rule through free and fair elections, a separation between the offices of President and Army chief, and reducing the army's role in domestic politics, while ensuring that the army's essential role in national security is properly institutionalized. Generous economic aid and properly targeted and conditioned military aid are part of this. The U.S. should not intervene in the tribal areas. And the United States urgently needs to try to strengthen and broaden the anti-terrorism consensus within Pakistan.

Pakistan Is Facing Three Challenges

Three short-term dramas are playing out in Pakistan. The first is a challenge to the basic authority of the government to keep order, best exemplified by the kidnapping and other lawless activities carried out by the Red Mosque leadership and their students. [President Pervez] Musharraf's decision to respond was welcomed by all but the most hard-line supporters of the militants, and briefly strengthened his position. Once the death toll became known, however, it was followed by a rash of suicide bombings, not just near the Afghan border but as far away as Karachi, leaving another 200 or so people dead. The extremist threat to Pakistan's government and society is still with us.

The second drama is the spillover from the conflict in Afghanistan. The demise of the agreement between the Pakistan government and the tribal leaders in Waziristan is the latest development on this front, although from my perspective that agreement never really went into operation, so its death should not be front-page news. This relates to the speculation about whether the United States will or should intervene militarily in the tribal areas to prevent Al-Qaeda from using them as a sanctuary.

The third drama stems from Musharraf's decision to suspend the Chief Justice last March [2007], which the Supreme Court has now overturned. The decision and the government's response, including the May riots in Karachi that left 40 people dead, shattered Musharraf's legitimacy and his popular support. It appears to have awakened considerable popular resentment against the army, and concern within the army.

The Supreme Court's ruling last week [July 2007] was a serious embarrassment to Musharraf. It also interferes with Musharraf's strategy of seeking reelection later this year, with the presidential election preceding the legislative elections, and with Musharraf retaining his post as Army chief. The legal provisions governing both the sequence of the elections and Musharraf's dual positions are complex and confusing, but it is clear that both will be challenged in the courts. Musharraf can no longer be confident that the courts will support him.

Pakistan Must Have a Legitimate Government

The United States needs Pakistan as a committed partner in the struggle against terrorism and insurgency, especially in the Pakistan/Afghanistan border region. It needs a Pakistan gov-

Pakistan Welcomes U.S. Assistance

How would Pakistan view an increase in economic assistance?

Pakistanis are acutely aware of the hiatus that occurred when USAID [U.S. Agency for International Development] left the country in the early 1990s, a departure that created a significant loss of trust between the US and Pakistan that remains today. Pakistanis would welcome increased assistance. What they would value more than increased assistance is a long-term commitment from the United States, a commitment that would reassure the Pakistanis that we will be their partner for many years to come.

Mark S. Ward,
statement before Senate Committee Foreign Relations,
June 25, 2008.

ernment that can keep order and has legitimacy, one that will not allow Pakistan to be used as a platform for insurgency or irredentism [trying to acquire neighboring regions or lands] in either Afghanistan or its nuclear-armed neighbor India.

My recommendations for U.S. policy focus on three things: support for Pakistan's return to elected, civilian government; dealing with Pakistan's frontier area; and military and economic aid.

Pakistan's political future matters profoundly to the future peace and governability of the region. The Supreme Court ruling has given us—and Pakistan—an opportunity to stand up for the rule of law. This is the only way to set Pakistan on the course toward "enlightened moderation" that many Pakistanis believe is their country's birthright. The United States has welcomed the Supreme Court decision. Accordingly, we need to make clear as events proceed that we expect the coming elections to be fully free and fair, with Musharraf choosing between the offices of president or army chief.

This may seem like an odd time for the United States to be taking a strong stand for moving back to a freely elected government and democratic institutions. This policy, however, is not just a reflection of American values. It also reflects a hard-nosed judgment about the relationship between the Pakistan army and the militants who threaten to destroy the progressive, modern Islamic character of the state that underpins real policy cooperation with the United States. In the past, when the Pakistani state has cracked down on extremist militants, the army has often pulled its punches, making sure that militant groups remained alive and available to work with them across Pakistan's tense borders in the future. That policy, I believe, is doomed to failure. Extremism cannot be kept half-contained in this fashion. It poses a mortal danger to Pakistan's domestic well-being. As long as the army remains in charge of policy, it is unlikely to treat the extremists as the enemy they are, and will not be able to end the domestic threat they pose. Doing this requires a committed political government, with full legitimacy. The army will of course play a critical role enforcing the government's policies and defending Pakistan. But this role needs to be anchored in a set of institutions in which elected political power is firmly in charge, and fully accountable.

Musharraf may be in trouble, but he is the leader in Pakistan today, so making this shift of emphasis without undermining his ability to make decisions will be tricky. Since he has said he wants to hold elections on time, and does not want to move toward a state of emergency, the policy I propose is in line with his stated goals. But it also recognizes that Pakistan's best shot at dealing with the danger of violent extremism comes from moving back to a government that enjoys full legitimacy.

The U.S. Should Not Intervene in Tribal Areas

Regarding the problem of the tribal areas, I strongly oppose direct US military intervention. I can think of no quicker way of turning all of Pakistan against the anti-terrorism goals that are so important to the United States, and turning the Pakistan army into a hostile force. Support for Pakistan's operations in the frontier area is another story: there we should be generous and creative.

But bringing the tribal areas under control is the work of a generation, and will require political and economic as well as military means. We do not understand the tribal society, its complex web of relationships with Pakistan and Afghanistan, and the fragile economy there, well enough to leave it in better shape than we found it. I support a major development program, despite the substantial risk that some of the money would go astray. Without jobs for the youth of the tribal areas, I don't see how one can begin the long task of bringing them into the government net. But let us be clear that this will not bear fruit for several years.

Providing Military and Economic Assistance

My final recommendation deals with assistance programs in Pakistan. I have long believed that we need to use our economic assistance to build a long term relationship with Pakistan. We should increase it relative to military assistance, and should hold it largely immune to the political ups and downs of the relationship. We should be programming our economic aid rather than giving it in cash or quasi-cash form, and we should be using our assistance to build up Pakistan's investment in its own people, in education and health.

Military assistance is also an important expression of our long-term commitment to the people of Pakistan, but here it is important to draw some distinctions we have not drawn in the past. Military sales should focus in the first instance on equipment that will help Pakistan with its vital counter-terrorism goals. Military sales that relate more to general defense upgrading should take a back seat, and should be contingent on Pakistan's effective performance in countering militant extremists, both along the Afghan border and elsewhere. If we continue to find that Pakistan's army is hedging its bets in Afghanistan and providing support for the Taliban, or for domestic militant groups, we should put this type of military sales on hold.

My other recommendation is more general. The administration has tended to speak of Musharraf whenever it is asked about policy toward Pakistan. I think we need to shift our emphasis to the whole of Pakistan. Obviously, leaders are important, especially in troubled countries at troubled times. But the sustainability of Pakistan's political system and its ability to grow new leaders are absolutely critical to the goal of combating terrorism that has been at the top of our list for the past six years. This means that we need the Pakistani political system—or as many parts of it as possible—to buy into the goal of eliminating extremist influence in Pakistan. Especially since the invasion of Iraq, this has become a very tough job in a country where public opinion now regards the United States as a country that "attacks Muslims." Hence my final recommendation. We need to listen to what Pakistanis are saying about their hopes for a better future for their country. If, as I suspect, there is widespread but amorphous sentiment for "enlightened moderation," we need to help strengthen and deepen that, and to show by our actions that this is where we want to go, together with Pakistan.

| *"The weakness of the U.S. bargaining position can be summed up in two words: 'fuel' and 'Afghanistan.'"*

The United States Does Not Have the Power to Change Pakistan's Policies

Robert Bryce

America's reliance on fuel from Pakistan means that the United States cannot adequately address the problem of terrorism, argues Robert Bryce in the following viewpoint. According to Bryce, because the U.S. military needs fuel from Pakistan in order to wage war in Afghanistan, the U.S. government cannot pressure Pakistan to investigate terrorist attacks. Furthermore, Bryce contends, the instability of Pakistan's government also makes it difficult for the U.S. military to uproot the Taliban presence in neighboring Afghanistan. Bryce is an author whose books include Gusher of Lies: The Dangerous Delusions of "Energy Independence."

As you read, consider the following questions:

1. According to data cited by Bryce, how many gallons of fuel does the U.S. military use in Afghanistan each day?

2. Why is the fuel flow from Azerbaijan especially precarious, in the author's view?

3. How much would fuel cost if the United States lost its supply from Pakistan, according to an analyst quoted by Bryce?

In the wake of the deadly terrorist attacks in Mumbai [November 2008], the U.S. government is pressuring Pakistan to investigate the incident that left more than 170 dead in India's largest city. After arriving Thursday [December 4, 2008] in Islamabad [Pakistan's capital], Secretary of State Condoleezza Rice demanded that the Pakistanis provide "robust" cooperation with the Indians to find the perpetrators. There has also been talk that the United States might suspend aid to Pakistan.

Don't believe it. America has little—if any—leverage with the Pakistani government. The weakness of the U.S. bargaining position can be summed up in two words: "fuel" and "Afghanistan."

According to the latest data from the Defense Energy Support Center, obtained under the Freedom of Information Act, the U.S. military is now consuming about 575,000 gallons of fuel per day in Afghanistan. And about half of that fuel is coming via truck from refineries in Pakistan. According to a presentation made by Army Col. Mark Olinger at the Defense Energy Support Center's biannual conference in Crystal City, Va., last April, the U.S. military in Afghanistan buys fuel from four different countries: Uzbekistan, Kazakhstan, Azerbaijan, and Pakistan. But it's the Pakistani refineries at Lahore, Karachi, and Attock that are the most essential.

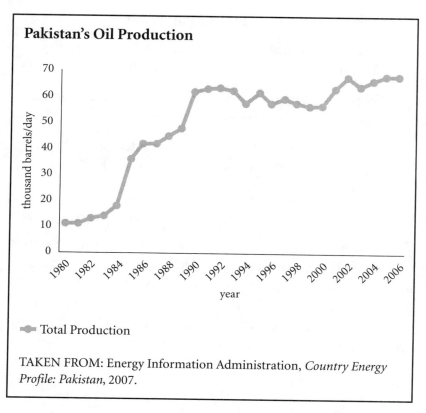

Pakistan's Oil Production

TAKEN FROM: Energy Information Administration, *Country Energy Profile: Pakistan*, 2007.

"The fuel flow into Afghanistan is like the supply coming in through the Burma Road," said Olinger, referring to the transportation challenges the British had during World War II in moving war materials into China via a treacherous mountainous road from Burma (now Myanmar).

Indeed, the logistics line that carries fuel from neighboring countries into Afghanistan is a critical weakness for American forces. And the fuel flow from Azerbaijan is particularly precarious. The fuel originates at a refinery in Baku, where it is loaded on rail cars that are then put onto barges that cross the Caspian Sea. When the cars land in Turkmenistan, they follow a circuitous rail route through Uzbekistan before they arrive at the Afghan border. The fuel is then transferred to trucks. In all, the fuel travels about 1,000 miles.

The fuel lines from Uzbekistan and Kazakhstan are recent additions to the U.S. military's supply routes for Afghanistan. For many months, the U.S. military had to rely on just two sources for fuel: Azerbaijan and Pakistan. And while the addition of the two "stans" is a positive development in terms of fuel security, both countries have uneasy relationships with the United States. The U.S. military was kicked out of Uzbekistan in 2005 and was allowed to return only earlier this year. Hydrocarbon-rich Kazakhstan has long attracted western interest, but the United States has been careful not to appear too accommodating to the country's autocratic leader, Nursultan Nazarbayev.

The Pakistanis fully understand the importance of the logistics line that carries fuel, food, and other supplies into Afghanistan. According to Olinger, all of the fuel trucked into Afghanistan goes through the northern Pakistani town of Peshawar, on the eastern side of the Khyber Pass. And the truck convoys out of Peshawar are a rich target for the warlords and other groups—some of which are allegedly linked to the Taliban—that operate in the region. In early November, 60 gunmen hijacked more than a dozen trucks carrying supplies for the U.S. military near the Khyber Pass. In September, according to Pakistan's *Daily Times* newspaper, the Pakistani government temporarily stopped all truck traffic on the road through the pass, citing security concerns. In April, a fuel truck wired with a bomb exploded near a customs post at Torkham on the Pakistan-Afghan border. And in March, a bomb attack destroyed 40 tanker trucks in the Khyber Agency near the border.

The U.S. military in Afghanistan would have a huge problem if the Pakistani government decided to close the supply route through the Khyber Pass or, perhaps worse, allowed local warlords and Taliban-affiliated groups to operate unfettered, thereby giving them license to hijack truck convoys at will.

If the U.S. loses its fuel supply line from Pakistan, "there's no way we can fly enough fuel into Afghanistan to supply the troops. We don't have enough tankers or enough personnel," says a senior civilian analyst at the Pentagon who asked that his name not be used because he was not authorized to speak to the press. "Even if we could do it the cost would be horrendous—maybe $40 to $50 per gallon of fuel delivered."

The U.S. military now has about 32,000 troops in Afghanistan. And while those soldiers may be hoping to uproot the Taliban and bring some measure of stability to Afghanistan, their key vulnerability involves one of the oldest problems in warfare: logistics. Those logistics are largely controlled by Pakistan, an unstable mess of a country that could devolve into chaos at any time. The latest hostilities between Pakistan and India only add to America's hypercomplicated diplomatic and logistical challenges in the region.

| "Mr. Obama must . . . produce a comprehensive strategy that addresses the political, military, and economic roots of the Pakistani threat."

The United States Needs to Engage More Fully with Pakistan

Arjun Parasher

In the following viewpoint, written before Barack Obama was sworn in as President of the United States, Arjun Parasher asserts that the incoming president needs to work more closely with Pakistan in order to combat terrorism. Parasher maintains that a partnership between the two nations would require counterterrorism training and equipment from the United States, along with political and economic aid that will create opportunities for young Pakistanis and undercut the Taliban's recruitment base. In Parasher's view, these steps will help destroy the militant base that threatens not only Pakistan but also its neighboring countries and the United States. Parasher is a Gates Scholar in international relations at the University of Cambridge.

Arjun Parasher, "Obama and Pakistan: The Need for Engagement," *Washington Times*, December 19, 2008, p. A25. Copyright © 2008 The Washington Times LLC. Reproduced by permission.

As you read, consider the following questions:

1. What is the greatest threat to U.S. national security, as stated by the author?

2. According to Parasher, why does Obama need to cultivate Pakistan's capacity to fight terrorism?

3. In the author's view, how can the U.S. eliminate anti-American sentiment in Pakistan?

Prior to the financial crisis, foreign policy and national security loomed as the greatest concerns to the American electorate in then-Sen. Barack Obama's candidacy for the presidency. However, the financial crisis quickly brought the economy, bailouts and stimulus packages to the forefront of policy debates. As a result, discussion of these potential weaknesses quietly faded into the background.

The recent [November 2008] terrorist attacks in Mumbai reminded us that the economy is not the only imminent threat that the president-elect must face. While the economic downturn has global etiologies, extremism seems to have found a common safe haven: Pakistan. Not only have Indian officials pointed to Pakistani-based Lashkar-e-Taiba as the culprit for the Mumbai attacks, but U.S. intelligence has also identified militancy within Pakistan as the greatest threat to U.S. national security. According to Joint Chiefs Chairman Michael G. Mullen, "If the United States is going to get hit, it's going to come out of [Pakistan's Federally Administered Tribal Areas (FATA)]." Pakistan does not represent a new hazard. When outgoing President [Bill] Clinton briefed incoming President [George W.] Bush on the six major threats to U.S. national security, three centered on the region: al Qaeda, Pakistan's support for the Taliban, and nuclear tensions between India and Pakistan. To make matters worse, in the post-[President Pervez] Musharraf era, the U.S. has been left without a prominent ally or a coherent strategy.

Obama Should Appoint a South Asia Envoy

Appoint a U.S. presidential South Asia envoy dedicated to the task of promoting better relations between Pakistan and Afghanistan and between Pakistan and India. Appointing a senior South Asia envoy would demonstrate that the U.S. is stepping up its regional diplomatic efforts to supplement its military operations in an effort to bring stability and security to Afghanistan. This diplomatic effort should seek to bring together Pakistani and Afghan leaders in joint initiatives that reduce conflict and build economic bridges between them. . . .

The envoy should also seek to reduce tensions between Pakistan and India, whose historical rivalry is increasingly being played out in Afghanistan. The U.S. can encourage initiatives that help these three countries develop a vested interest in each other's stability and security. The recent opening of a road that crosses the Line of Control that divides Indian and Pakistani Kashmir is one example of the kind of confidence-building measures that are so badly needed in the region.

Lisa Curtis and Walter Lohman,
"Stiffening Pakistan's Resolve Against Terrorism,"
December 16, 2008.

Pakistan Is the Key to Long-term Security

According to the Bush administration, militant groups have consistently attempted to infiltrate Pakistan's nuclear laboratories—a disturbing fact, considering that just this past August [2008] militants were able to execute a devastating attack on the Pakistan Ordnance Factories, a weapons complex previously believed to be impregnable. Such anarchy is especially troubling, given Pakistan's vital role in stemming violence in Afghanistan. With inflation at 25 percent and literacy rates barely reaching 50 percent, Pakistan's problems are deep-rooted and complicated. However, one fact remains clear: Pakistan's future holds the key to the long-term security of not only Afghanistan, but also that of the U.S. and India.

Yet, in regards to this threat, the U.S. election and transition process have revealed only that President-elect Obama is committed to more troops in Afghanistan and believes in America's right to pursue terrorists across borders. More is needed. Mr. Obama must utilize the transition period to produce a comprehensive strategy that addresses the political, military, and economic roots of the Pakistani threat.

First, he must cultivate Pakistani political will and capacity to combat terrorism with a joint strategy. The logic is simple: as the capacity to act increases, the costs of action decline, reducing the threshold of political will required to initiate that action. To summon political will, the fight against terrorism must be translated into terms that emphasize Pakistan's interests, not those of the U.S. The Pakistani people cherish democracy: Mr. Musharraf's dictatorship, prolonged presidency, and U.S. support of it represented a threat to democracy; the motivation to eliminate this threat has served as the only unifying political element in recent times. As such, the U.S. must illustrate the threat that terrorism poses to democracy to both the Pakistani leadership and public, as a means of galvanizing political will and unifying a fragile government.

Given that the Pakistani military's last foray into the tribal areas resulted in humiliating defeat and internationally condemned peace accords, capacity must be improved through joint U.S.-Pakistan counter-terrorism operations. Furthermore, the U.S. must provide counter-terrorism training and equipment, while demanding accountability. Resource allocation has shown the opposite intent: The Bush administration recently attempted to shift $230 million out of the allocated

$300 million in military aid to Pakistan from counter-terrorism toward upgrading F-16s, a clear attempt to appease the Pakistani military establishment, and its fixation with India, with little if any practical utility for the war on terror. Congress must resist further misdirected appeasements.

Pakistan Needs More than Military Support

Lastly, to avoid the mistakes of the past, the U.S. must move beyond military support to tackle Pakistan's economic and political challenges. Anti-U.S. sentiment and the engrained rivalry with India can only be wiped clean with new economic and political opportunities for young Pakistanis, particularly those living in FATA and the North-West Frontier Province. A recent Senate bill to provide $7.5 billion for development projects over the next five years, sponsored by Sens. Joseph Biden and Richard Lugar, is a start. In addition, public opinion must be buoyed by a political engagement that cultivates local leaders and addresses civilian concerns. These initiatives would severely undercut the Taliban's recruitment base: poor, disenfranchised Pashtuns.

To ensure that his perceived foreign policy weakness, while forgotten at home, does not remain abroad, Mr. Obama owes it to the American people to tackle Pakistan's militant base at its roots. Our security and freedom depend on it.

Periodical Bibliography

Michael Fathers "No Easy Way Out," *New Statesman*, July 7, 2008.

Michael Hirsh "Our Man in Pakistan," *Washington Monthly*, January/February 2006.

Nicholas D. Kristoff "It Takes a School, Not Missiles," *New York Times*, July 13, 2008.

Mark Landler and Elisabeth Bumiller "Now, U.S. Sees Pakistan as a Cause Distinct from Afghanistan," *New York Times*, May 1, 2009.

Anatol Lieven "Do No Harm," *National Interest*, March/April 2008.

Mustafa Malik "Pakistan: Can U.S. Policy Save the Day?" *Middle East Policy*, Summer 2009.

Tara McKelvey "Our Man in Kabul," *American Prospect*, April 2009.

Thomas Omestad "How Nuclear-Armed Rivals Pakistan and India Will Test Obama," *U.S. News & World Report*, January 7, 2009.

Barnett R. Rubin and Ahmed Rashid "From Great Game to Grand Bargain," *Foreign Affairs*, November/December 2008.

Michael Rubin "Sixty Miles from the Capital," *Weekly Standard*, May 11, 2009.

Judith Stone "Teach a Girl, Save the World," *Good Housekeeping*, June 2009.

Stephen Zunes "Pakistan's Dictatorships and the United States," *Foreign Policy in Focus*, November 11, 2007.

CHAPTER 4

What Is the Future of Pakistan?

Chapter Preface

For most Americans, the most recognizable figure in Pakistani politics was Benazir Bhutto. She served as the nation's prime minister from 1988 to 1990 and again from 1993 to 1996, both terms ending prematurely when she was dismissed from office by Pakistan's president (in the first instance, Ghulam Ishaq Khan, and in the second instance, Farooq Leghari). After living in exile in London for nine years, she returned to Pakistan in 2007 with the aim of becoming prime minister for the third time. However, her comeback was cut short when she was assassinated on December 27, 2007.

Bhutto's death raised questions about the political future of Pakistan. Her widower, Asif Ali Zardari, took over as leader of the Pakistan People's Party and as of this writing was the president of Pakistan. Despite the continued influence of her family, political commentators disagree over whether Bhutto would have brought stability to Pakistan had she survived and been reelected.

Supporters of Bhutto assert that her death made it more difficult for Pakistan to meet its economic and political challenges. In an article for *USA Today*, published the day after her death, Zafar M. Sheikh and Paul Wiseman wrote, "Despite two tenures as prime minister that ended prematurely amid allegations of corruption, Bhutto offered a unique, perhaps irreplaceable mix: She was a popular, charismatic speaker capable of charming the Western world." Others maintain, however, that Bhutto's history of corruption meant she could never truly bring political stability to Pakistan. Among her critics was *New York Post* columnist Ralph Peters, who asserted that Bhutto's two terms as prime minister were marked by the worsening of life for regular Pakistanis. He wrote, "During her years as prime minister, Pakistan went backward, not forward."

The assassination of Bhutto had a significant impact on Pakistani politics and could continue to reverberate for years to come. In the following chapter, the contributors debate the economic, political, and social future of Pakistan.

| "*Pakistan, even though it is sixty years old, faces some of the same nation-building challenges that far younger, less mature countries do.*"

Pakistan Faces Political Instability

Richard N. Haass, interviewed by Bernard Gwertzman

In the following viewpoint, Richard N. Haass opines that Pakistan will likely become politically unstable as a result of the assassination of former prime minister Benazir Bhutto and parliamentary elections that are unlikely to unify the nation. He contends that these political problems will make it more difficult for Pakistan to address internal security threats and could lead to a deterioration in public order. Haass concludes that the future of Pakistan is messy and poses a threat not only to that nation but also to Afghanistan, India, and the United States. Haass is the president of the Council on Foreign Relations, while Bernard Gwertzman is a consulting editor. The Council on Foreign Relations is a nonpartisan think tank that provides analysis on world events and American foreign policy.

Bernard Gwertzman and Richard N. Haass, "Interview: Pakistan Faces 'Prolonged Difficult Future,'" CFR.org, January 2, 2008, www.cfr.org/publication/15150. Copyright © 2008 by the Council on Foreign Relations. All rights reserved. Reproduced by permission.

As you read, consider the following questions:

1. What does Haass view as a "disheartening reminder" of the limits of democracy in Pakistan?

2. Why does Haass find it interesting that President Musharraf has deployed the Pakistani army prior to the elections?

3. What are Pakistan's military officers preoccupied with, according to Haass?

B*ernard Gwertzman: Please summarize what you see happening in Pakistan since the assassination of Benazir Bhutto last month [December 2007].*

[Richard N. Haass:] There have been at least four important developments. The first is that the government of President Pervez Musharraf seems to have reacted to the domestic and international criticism about its handling of the assassination, including the continued uncertainty on exactly what was the cause of her death, and more importantly who was behind it. The fact that it now looks as if Scotland Yard [Britain's Metropolitan Police] will be involved is an important development because there is precious little domestic or international confidence in the ability of the government to carry out a fair and impartial investigation. So potentially this is a good development.

Secondly, you had the meeting of Ms. Bhutto's PPP [Pakistan People's Party] and the emergence of a new leadership, which, in fact, is not terribly new. This is in many ways a disheartening reminder of how little democracy there is in Pakistan. This is an indication that Pakistani politics are more familial and feudal than they are representative.

Internal Security Is a Serious Concern

You are talking about the naming of her 19-year old son, Bilawal, as the new titular head of the party and her husband, Asif

Ali Zardari—who has the nickname of "Mr. 10 Percent" for the kickbacks he allegedly received when he was in government—as the real leader?

Exactly. This is again a disquieting reminder of how distant party politics in Pakistan are from democratic politics.

The other two points?

Thirdly, the decision by President Musharraf to deploy the army around the country in the run-up to the elections, and possibly beyond, is interesting for several reasons. It tells us that both Musharraf and the leadership of the army are worried about internal security. This deployment is not something they would do lightly because it puts the army precisely in the position the army has tried to avoid, which is to be the provider of order. It's risky for the army not simply because it has not fared terribly well against the terrorists to date, but also because it possibly puts it in a position where it has to deal with civil disturbance. Therefore, it potentially places the army in positions where both the loyalty of its troops and its legitimacy in public eyes could come into question. So for Musharraf to do that or to agree to it is a great risk because if things begin to deteriorate it's quite possible that the army would decide it was better to oust Musharraf than to allow its own legitimacy and unity to be compromised.

The fourth development is the announcement that elections will be postponed for some six weeks until February 18 [2008]. My view is that that is a reasonable decision, given the need to provide security, which is an essential prerequisite for an election campaign. I also think that having a specific date set is a good thing rather than leaving the date open-ended.

So if you were writing a memo now for the Secretary of State would you suggest that Washington should give a positive evaluation of the speech and such specifics as the elections postponement?

To me the question is not so much whether the United States should have a positive or negative take on it so much as

A Government Facing Many Problems

Pakistan's leaders seem to be in denial about the seriousness of the [Taliban] threat. In December [2008], amid reports of militant atrocities in Swat and nighttime attacks on elite schools in Peshawar, President Asif Ali Zardari told a group of parliamentarians that the situation in the North West Frontier Province was "improving." Frustrating as this is, it is in some sense a plausible response for a government facing so many problems on so many fronts, with so little ability to counter them. Taliban violence, heightened tensions with India, an economy hobbled by a global recession and riots over power outages at home have left the government staggering under the weight of a seemingly unbearable burden.

Vanessa Gezart,
"Insurgency Takes Heavy Toll on Pakistani Police,"
St. Petersburg Times, *February 15, 2009.*

the United States essentially not having much influence over what was announced or over what will come. That to me is the larger truth of Pakistan, for better or worse—and more often for worse. The future of Pakistan will be determined by Pakistani rather than by American policy. But I take your question. Musharraf deserves conditional support and the United States ought to endorse the decision to hold elections by mid-February; it ought also to state its definition of what would be free and fair and legitimate elections. Independent American organizations, I believe, should offer assistance to the Pakistanis. And at some point, the United States also needs to make clear it is ready to continue aid and to reorient the aid so that it's more closely connected to the anti-terrorist mission rather than to a general buildup of the Pakistani military.

Pakistan's Army Has the Wrong Mission

On the question of the terrorists in Pakistan: They are linked to the terrorists in Afghanistan, the Taliban, and al-Qaeda groups. There doesn't seem to be much progress in coordinating efforts since the two countries dislike each other so.

You're right to say there is little love lost between the two governments. But Pakistan's problems in confronting the internal threat go way beyond any lack of coordination with Afghanistan. What you have in Pakistan is a fundamental lack of state capacity. Pakistan, even though it is sixty years old, faces some of the same nation-building challenges that far younger, less mature countries do. This recent talk about the creation of a Frontier Corps in the western part of the country resembles the challenges we are facing both in Iraq and in Afghanistan, which is the building up of relevant paramilitary capacities of a state. It's further proof that the Pakistani army is not well-suited to this mission and much of U.S. aid up until now has not contributed significantly to Pakistan's ability to deal with its real challenges.

Pakistan's army has really been built to fight a war with India, hasn't it?

Too much of what motivates Pakistani military officers is preoccupation with India, when the reality is that India is not a strategic challenge to Pakistan. Pakistan does not face an external threat in any meaningful way. On a day-to-day basis, the real threat to Pakistan's sovereignty, to its viability, and to its security and prosperity, comes from within. To the extent that disorder is fed from without, it is not coming from Delhi [India's capital] but from places like Afghanistan or from so-called 'volunteers' from other places in the Muslim world.

Democracy Is Not in Pakistan's Immediate Future

Prior to Ms. Bhutto's assassination, the polls seemed to predict her party gaining a plurality and no party winning a clear majority. How do you think the new government will work out after next month's elections for the parliament?

My guess is that we're heading toward an electoral outcome in which it is quite possible there is no clear winner. We could be facing a future in which you have a coalition government with two or more parties, which means you would have shared power both within the parliament and between the parliament and the presidency, i.e. with Mr. Musharraf, as well as among the parliament, the presidency, the military, and the courts. My sense is that we're looking at a period of more distributed or shared power within Pakistan. My prediction is that with or without President Musharraf in place, we need to anticipate considerable drift, by which I mean you will have constant political jockeying and skirmishing, lower economic growth rates, and probably a messy security situation in which any progress vis-à-vis the Taliban or al-Qaeda or local extremists is at best fitful. That to me is the most likely scenario. One wouldn't describe as reassuring. It is also possible to imagine worse scenarios in which public order breaks down. Initially, if that were the case, the army would probably decide the time had come to retire President Musharraf.

But even in a post-Musharraf situation, one could imagine where public order deteriorated and the real threat to Pakistan became a version of state failure, or one in which the extremists or terrorists could gain even more sway. That to me is the more troublesome possibility. I would say, however, it is less likely than what I described as "drift."

You don't see democracy emerging as a result of all this.

The best and arguably most likely course is a degree of messiness: what would politely be called shared political power and potentially a government of national unity, but in reality, what would be contested political power and a government of national disunity. In those circumstances it is hard to see effective action being taken against those who readily use force against the government. But to answer your question, no, I don't see Pakistan likely to come together in a form of a highly efficient democracy. I just don't see the building blocks there at present.

I see a prolonged difficult future in a country that is quite messy. That is bad for the struggle against terrorism; it is bad for Afghanistan; it's bad for Indians if they have an unstable neighbor; and obviously it is bad for the United States for all of the above.

| "Almost everyone I talked to was sure that democracy was the best answer to Pakistan's problems."

Pakistan Can Achieve Democracy

William Dalrymple

William Dalrymple asserts in the following viewpoint that Pakistanis want the right to choose their own rulers. He further states that while Pakistan may have its economic and political problems, it is a much more stable nation than its critics believe. According to Dalrymple, the feudalism that has typified Pakistani politics in the past is gradually disappearing as people begin to see democracy as the answer to the nation's problems. Dalrymple is a writer and historian.

As you read, consider the following questions:

1. What is the central question facing Pakistan, as stated by the author?

2. According to Dalrymple, what are elections in Pakistan actually about?

3. What was noteworthy about the winning candidates in the Jhang district, as observed by the author?

William Dalrymple, "Pakistan Reborn?" *New Statesman*, February 25, 2008, pp. 26–28. Copyright © 2008 New Statesman, Ltd. Reproduced by permission.

It has not been a good year for Pakistan. President [Pervez] Musharraf's sacking of the chief justice last spring [2007], the lawyers' protests that rumbled on throughout the summer and the bloody storming of the Red Mosque in June, followed by a wave of hideous suicide bombings, all gave the impression of a country stumbling from bloody crisis to bloody crisis. By the autumn it had grown even worse. The military defeats suffered by the Pakistani army at the hands of pro-Taliban rebels in Waziristan, the declaration of a state of emergency and, finally, the assassination of Benazir Bhutto [December 2007] led many to predict that Pakistan was stumbling towards full-scale civil war and possibly even disintegration.

All this has of course been grist for the mill for the Pakistan-bashers. Martin Amis, typical of the current rash of instant experts on Islam, wrote recently: "We may wonder how the Islamists feel when they compare India to Pakistan, one a burgeoning democratic superpower, the other barely distinguishable from a failed state." In the run-up to the elections, the *Washington Post*, among many other commentators, was predicting that the poll would lead to a major international crisis.

It Is Time to Reassess Pakistan

That the election went ahead with no more violence and ballot-rigging than is considered customary in south Asian polls, and that a new government will apparently come to power peacefully, unopposed by Musharraf or the army, should now give pause for thought and a calmer reassessment of the country that many have long written off as a basket case.

Certainly, there is no question that during the past few years, and more pressingly since the death of Benazir Bhutto on 27 December last year, Pakistan has been struggling with an existential crisis. At the heart of this lay the central question: what sort of country did Pakistanis want? Did they want a western-style liberal democracy, as envisaged by Pakistan's founder, Muhammad Ali Jinnah? An Islamic republic like Mullah Omar's Afghanistan? Or a military-ruled junta of the sort created by Generals Ayub Khan, Zia and Musharraf, and which has ruled Pakistan for 34 of its 60 years of existence?

Pakistanis Want to Determine Their Future

That question now seems to have been resolved, at least temporarily. Like most other people given the option, Pakistanis clearly want the ability to choose their own rulers, and to determine their own future. The country I saw over the past few days on a long road trip from Lahore in the Punjab down through rural Sindh to Karachi was not a failed state, nor anything even approaching the "most dangerous country in the world".

It is true that frequent shortages of electricity made the country feel a bit like Britain during the winter of discontent, and I was told at one point that I should not continue along certain roads near the Bhutto stronghold of Larkana as there were dacoits (highwaymen) ambushing people after dark. But by and large, the countryside I passed through was calm, and not obviously less prosperous-looking than its subcontinental neighbour. It was certainly a far cry from the terminal lawlessness and instability of post-occupation Iraq or Afghanistan.

The infrastructure of the country is still in many ways better than that of India, and Pakistan still has the best airports and road network in the region. As for the economy, it may be in difficulties, with fast-rising inflation and shortages of gas, electricity and flour; but over the past few years the Pakistani economy has been growing almost as strongly as that of India. You can see the effects everywhere: in 2003 the country had fewer than three million cellphone users; today there are almost 50 million. Car ownership has been increasing at roughly 40 per cent a year since 2001; foreign direct investment has risen from $322m [million] in 2001 to $3.5bn [billion] in 2006.

Pakistan is clearly not a country on the verge of civil war. Certainly it is a country at the crossroads, with huge economic and educational problems, hideous inequalities and serious unresolved questions about its future. There is much confusion and disillusion. There is also serious civil unrest, suicide bombings and an insurgency spilling out of the tribal areas on the Afghan border. But judging by the conversations I had, it is also a resilient country that now appears to recognise democracy as its best hope. On my recent travels I found an almost unanimous consensus that the mullahs [religious leaders] should keep to their mosques and the military should return to their barracks, like their Indian counterpart. Much violence and unrest no doubt lie ahead. But Pakistan is not about to fall apart.

Elections in south Asia are treated by the people of the region as operating on a quite different basis from those in the west. In Pakistan, as in India, elections are not primarily about ideology or manifesto promises; instead, they are really about power and patronage.

Traditional Pakistani Politics Are Breaking Down

For most voters, elections are about choosing candidates who can outbid their rivals by making a string of local promises that the electors hope they will honour once they get into office. Typically, a parliamentary candidate will go to a village and make promises or give money to one of the village elders, who will then distribute it among his bradari, or clan, which will then vote for the candidate en bloc [as a group]. To win an election, the most important thing is to win over the elder of the most powerful clan in each village. As well as money, the elder might ask for various favours: a new tarmac road to the village or gas connections for his cousins. All this costs the candidate a considerable sum of money, which it is understood he must then recoup through corruption when he gets into office; this is why corruption is rarely an important election issue in Pakistan: instead, it is believed to be be an indispensable part of the system.

According to the conventional wisdom in Pakistan, only one thing can overrule loyalty to a clan, and that is loyalty to a zamindar (feudal landowner). Democracy has never thrived in Pakistan in part because landowning has historically been the social base from which politicians emerge, especially in rural areas. Benazir Bhutto was from a feudal family in Sindh; so is Asif Zardari, her husband and current co-chairman of the Pakistan People's Party (PPP), as also is Makhdoom Amin Fahim, the most likely candidate for prime minister. The educated middle class—which in India gained control in 1947—and even more so the rural peasantry, are still largely excluded from Pakistan's political process. There are no Pakistani equivalents of Indian peasant leaders such as Laloo Prasad Yadav, the village cowherd-turned-former chief minister of Bihar, or [Kumari] Mayawati, the Dalit (untouchable) leader and current chief minister of Uttar Pradesh.

Instead, in many of the more backward parts of Pakistan, the local feudal landowner could usually expect his people to vote for his chosen candidate. As the writer Ahmed Rashid put it, "In some constituencies if the feudals put up their dog as a candidate, that dog would get elected with 99 per cent of the vote."

Such loyalty could be enforced. Many of the biggest zamindars are said to have private prisons, and most of them have private armies. In the more remote and lawless areas there is also the possibility that the zamindars and their thugs will bribe or threaten polling agents, then simply stuff the ballot boxes with thousands of votes for themselves.

Yet this is now clearly beginning to change, and this change has been given huge impetus by the national polls. The election results show that the old stranglehold on Pakistani politics that used to reduce national polls to a kind of elective

Key Developments in Pakistan

Powerful developments are propelling [Pakistani democracy] along. The first is a decline in the army's popularity after the rule of [Pervez] Musharraf, and in its morale after losses in the unpopular campaign against the Pakistani Taliban, which has made the military reluctant to intervene directly against the will of the people. . . .

[Another] is the complete transformation of the country's media and communications industries, with dozens of independent television channels and tens of millions of new mobile phone connections creating, in effect, a giant electronic public forum.

Mohsin Hamid,
"Pakistan Is Being Shaped by Popular Will As Never Before,"
The Guardian, *March 17, 2009.*

feudalism may finally be beginning to break down. In Jhang district of the rural Punjab, for example, as many as ten of the 11 winning candidates are from middle-class backgrounds: sons of revenue officers, senior policemen, functionaries in the civil bureaucracy and so on, rather than the usual zamindars. . . .

If the power of Pakistan's feudals is beginning to be whittled away, in the aftermath of these unexpectedly peaceful elections there remain two armed forces that can still affect the future of democracy in the country.

Military Forces Could Threaten Democracy

Though the religious parties were routed in the election, especially in the North-West Frontier where the ruling religious MMA [Muttahida Majlis-e-Amal] alliance was wiped out by the secular ANP [Awami National Party], their gun-wielding brothers in Waziristan are not in retreat. In recent months these militants have won a series of notable military victories over the Pakistani army, and spread their revolt within the settled areas of Pakistan proper.

The two assassination attempts on Benazir—the second one horribly successful—and the three recent attacks on Musharraf are just the tip of the iceberg. Every bit as alarming is the degree to which the jihadis [those espousing "holy war"] now control much of the north-west of Pakistan, and the Swat Valley is still smouldering as government troops and jihadis loyal to the insurgent leader Maulana Fazllullah—aka "Mullah Radio" vie for control. At the moment, the government seems to have won back the area, but the insurgent leaders have all escaped and it remains to be seen how far the new government can stem this growing rebellion.

The second force that has shown a remarkable ability to ignore, or even reverse, the democratic decisions of the Pakistani people is of course the army. Even though Musharraf's political ally the PML-Q [Pakistan Muslim League (Quaid)] has been heavily defeated, leaving him vulnerable to impeachment by the new parliament, the Pakistani army is still formidably powerful. Normally countries have an army; in Pakistan, as in Burma, the army has a country. In her recent book *Military, Inc*, the political scientist Ayesha Siddiqa attempted to put figures on the degree to which the army controls Pakistan irrespective of who is in power.

Siddiqa estimated, for example, that the army now controls business assets of roughly $20bn and a third of all heavy manufacturing in the country; it also owns 12 million acres of public land and up to 7 per cent of Pakistan's private assets. Five giant conglomerates, known as "welfare foundations", run thousands of businesses, ranging from street-corner petrol pumps and sprawling industrial plants to cement and dredging to the manufacture of cornflakes.

As one human rights activist put it to me, "The army is into every business in this country. Except hairdressing." The army has administrative assets, too. According to Siddiqa, military personnel have "taken over all and every department in the bureaucracy—even the civil service academy is now headed by a major general, while the National School of Public Policy is run by a lieutenant general. The military have completely taken over not just the bureaucracy but every arm of the executive."

But, for all this power, Musharraf has now comprehensively lost the support of his people—a dramatic change from the situation even three years ago when a surprisingly wide cross-section of the country seemed prepared to tolerate military rule. The new army chief, General Ashfaq Kayani, who took over when Musharraf stepped down from his military role last year, seems to recognise this and has issued statements about his wish to pull the army back from civilian life, ordering his soldiers to stay out of politics and give up jobs in the bureaucracy.

Though turnout in the election was low, partly due to fear of suicide bombings, almost everyone I talked to was sure that democracy was the best answer to Pakistan's problems, and believed that neither an Islamic state nor a military junta [government run by a group of military leaders] would serve their needs so well. The disintegration of the country, something being discussed widely only a week ago, now seems a distant prospect. Rumours of Pakistan's demise, it seems, have been much exaggerated.

> "We hope that the women elected into assemblies and the national parliament will move to continue progress of women's rights and institutionalise changes."

Pakistan Should Make Efforts to Improve Women's Rights

Farida Shaheed, interviewed by Rochelle Jones

In the following viewpoint, Farida Shaheed details how Pakistani women are learning about and expanding their rights. According to Shaheed, organizations such as Shirkat Gah are working with policymakers in Pakistan to improve the rights of women and human rights as a whole. While Shaheed is concerned about how the current political situation in Pakistan will affect women's rights, she hopes that a democratically elected government will help the cause. Shaheed is a founding member of the Women's Action Forum and a sociologist who has extensively researched women's issues. Rochelle Jones interviewed Shaheed for the Association for Women's Rights in Development (AWID), which is an international organization that aims to advance the rights of women.

As you read, consider the following questions:

1. In Shaheed's view, why is it the responsibility of urban middle-class women to advance the cause of women's rights in Pakistan?

2. What is the motto of the women's rights organization Shirkat Gah, as stated by Shaheed?

3. How does Shaheed view Benazir Bhutto's widower, Asif Ali Zardari?

A WID [Association for Women's Rights in Development]: Women in Pakistan are subject to some of the most horrendous rights violations worldwide. How are women mobilising for gender equality and women's rights?

Farida Shaheed (FS): Pakistan is a country of great contrasts—so it seems that we have people living in different centuries rather than just locations, with different rules and constraints as well as opportunities. Constraints, rules and opportunities also vary enormously by class background. So while we have strong articulate women's advocates in large cities, the challenge is how to expand and link up with women in different classes and rural locations as well as in smaller towns, making sure that their voices are heard, their concerns articulated.

With Pakistan being under military rule longer than civilian rule, this increases the level of risk to activists. The severity of these risks varies with class and it has fallen to the urban middle class women with lesser risks to security and person to advance the movement. Given the numerically small number of activists, there has been a tendency to focus attention on the state: its actions and policies and laws (often trying to deny women their rights).

Reaching out to Women

While state policies and laws are critical of course, women on the whole interact very little with the state, and are obliged to negotiate rights through the . . . level of family, parallel adjudication and governance structures that impact their lives most immediately.

The fewer women who know about and enjoy state given rights, the more vulnerable these rights are to being overturned by dictators. Hence many organisations like Shirkat Gah have started 'outreach' programmes: that is, programmes to reach women in different village and urban locations. This has expanded the base of women's rights activists and the movement as a whole.

Equally we try and ensure that international debates are shared with women in communities we work with and that their concerns and demands are articulated at the national and supra national levels. Secondly, the women's rights movement has built strong links with human rights groups and actors within Pakistan to make common cause. This has helped to expand the movement and has also brought women's issues onto the agenda of the general human rights movement. Thirdly, we have linked up with women's rights groups and movements in the region and globally.

Democracy Helps Women's Rights

AWID: In your opinion, how closely related are women's rights and democracy in Pakistan? How do women's organisations influence government decisions?

FS: While democracy is not a panacea [cure-all]; our experience is that democracy and democratic spaces (not merely electoral processes, but inclusion in decision-making) support women's rights while dictatorial dispensations (whether military or civilian) tend to undermine women's rights. We believe many of the problems confronting women are common with other citizens and that there is therefore a need to link up with and support each other for a better society.

Shirkat Gah's motto is Women's Empowerment for Social Justice and Social Justice for Women's Empowerment. For this, we work towards strengthening women as rights claimants and also work to ensure that duty bearers are better attuned to women's needs and improve the delivery of state rights and services.

Organisations have different strategies that include: lobbying with policy-makers for improved laws and policies and regulations, projects etc.—often done in alliance with other women's groups and also human rights groups in general; using opportunities tied to national decision-making such as the 5 year development plans, national policy for women; and reporting to the UN [United Nations] system as a means to raise issues and press for change.

We have worked with parliamentarians to table and then to negotiate bills into acts by providing background materials and research, bringing in required expertise, meeting with standing committees of parliament—but we also use the mushrooming of new independent cable television networks and FM radio stations to get our opinions to a wider set of people—we also use newspaper articles (but less systematically). Finally and always there are public protests and demonstrations. Less frequently we have used street and interactive theatre to catalyse thinking and debates within communities resistant to change.

The Impact of Bhutto's Death

AWID: There have been some major political upheavals in Pakistan in the past 12 months, including the assassination of Benazir Bhutto [December 2007] and the resignation of [President Pervez] Musharraf [August 2008]. How did the assassination of Bhutto impact the women's rights movement?

FS: The assassination of Benazir was a blow to women in Pakistan as a whole, she symbolized for many the full potential of women here—that women could become the head of government.

Violence Against Women and Girls Is Growing

In December [2006], Pakistan's Parliament passed the Women's Protection Bill, which amended the Hudood Ordinances, a set of religious laws long considered discriminatory toward women. But by shifting the laws from religious codes to secular ones, the bill unleashed widespread political discontent. . . .

Recent events suggest a growing arc of violence against women and girls. In the North West Frontier province, at least three girls' schools have been bombed, and threats circulated by pamphlets have directed female health workers to leave the area.

David Montero,
"Violent Debate on Women's Rights in Pakistan,"
Christian Science Monitor, *March 6, 2007.*

Although Benazir was not a women's rights activist as such, many in the women's movement were profoundly shocked and upset. She was a defiant woman and a progressive force for democracy in very troubled times for the country. Her acceding to power had immense symbolic impact: this assumption by a woman of democratically elected power reverberated throughout society—resulting in an immediate easing of the social atmosphere, an invisible but palpable lifting of social constraints and a greater respect for women's rights demands than otherwise. It was in this sense that her assassination was a tragedy for the women and women's movement in Pakistan.

AWID: What are your thoughts on the recent election of her widower, Asif Ali Zardari as President? What is the potential for his appointment to impact women's rights?

FS: With the PPP [Pakistan People's Party] now in control of the presidency as well as the parliament, we hope that it will put women squarely on the agenda in a progressive way. However, politics in the past have shown that women's rights are all too often sacrificed in the bargaining chip in the larger game of political manoeuvring and alliance building. The fear of such bargaining is always present and remains. Zardari is an unknown entity politically speaking, leaving many wary of backdoor arrangements—however he was democratically elected. It is too soon to say what impact it will have on women.

Achieving the Goals of the Women's Rights Movement

AWID: What are the hopes of the women's rights movement with these recent changes and renewed hopes for democracy?

FS: We can only hope that the democratically elected government moves on with a strong decision to counter the right wing Talibanisation of the country by armed extremists using Islam. We hope that this brings peace so the government can concentrate on the very dire economic situation. We hope that the women elected into assemblies and the national parliament will move to continue progress of women's rights and institutionalise changes.

AWID: How do you aim to achieve your goals?

FS: Women's rights activists continue to work with the parliamentarians, most recently in commenting on and suggesting improvements to the Domestic Violence Bill and other issues. We continue to mobilise women and public opinion to change practices harmful to women. We continue to support all democratic forces, most especially the lawyers' community in their struggle for a free independent judiciary, and link up with diverse alliances and coalitions fighting for social justice for all.

| "There is little doubt that if extremists succeed in getting nuclear materials, they will not hesitate in using them."

Pakistan Is at Risk from Nuclear Weapons

Pervez Hoodbhoy

Pervez Hoodbhoy argues in the following viewpoint that Pakistan's possession of nuclear weapons could backfire on the nation. According to Hoodbhoy, Pakistan may believe that its weapons deter threats from India. However, he contends, these weapons could be stolen by Islamic militants and used against Pakistani citizens. Further, notes Hoodbhoy, extremists could develop their own weapons with the assistance of employees at Pakistani weapons laboratories. Hoodbhoy is a professor and chair of the department of physics at Quaid-e-Azam University in Islamabad, Pakistan.

As you read, consider the following questions:

1. As explained by the author, in what year does Pakistan's nuclear weapons story begin?

Pervez Hoodbhoy, "The Charm Fades: The Country Most at Risk from Pakistan's Bomb Could Be Pakistan Itself (Nuclear Weapons)," *New Internationalist*, June 2008. Copyright © 2008 New Internationalist Magazine. Reproduced by permission.

2. Why did tensions rise between India and Pakistan in December 2001, according to Hoodbhoy?

3. In the view of the author, what are the most likely targets if Pakistani extremists get their hands on nuclear weapons?

It is 10 years since Pakistan's atomic tests. But there is none of the chest-thumping, trumpet-blowing nuclear triumphalism of a decade ago. As the country reels under almost daily bomb blasts and suicide attacks by Islamic fundamentalists, the mood is downbeat. Only a few fireglass models of the Chaghi nuclear test site remain from yesteryears, and schoolchildren no longer wear free badges embellished with little mushroom clouds. Missile replicas, once prominent in public squares and major intersections, are almost gone.

Nevertheless, nuclear weapons are not on the way out in South Asia. India's enthusiasm for the bomb remains high and drives the subcontinent's nuclear race. In spite of remarkably good relations currently, the two adversaries are frantically producing more fissile materials and warheads, as well as extending, improving, and testing their intermediate-range ballistic missiles.

The History of Nuclear Weapons in Pakistan

That's not how it was supposed to be. Pro-establishment analysts in India and Pakistan, in a surprising show of solidarity, had long pooh-poohed the notion of nuclear racing. South Asians were not, they said, like the dumb, compulsive Soviets and Americans who had produced an unimaginable 70,000 nukes at the peak. At a conference in Chicago in 1992, the hawkish Indian strategist, K Subramanyam, snapped at me that 'arms racing is a Cold War concept invented by the Western powers and totally alien to sub-continental thinking'.

Minimal deterrence was the mantra of those days. The late General K Sunderji, chief of India's army, loved nukes. But he also insisted that a few was plenty: India needed only a dozen or so Hiroshima-sized city-busters, and so did Pakistan! In a chance encounter in 1995, when I introduced myself to him as a Pakistani nuclear physicist, his eyes lit up. He hugged me warmly, insisting that a happy Pakistan must have nukes. I did not have the heart to tell him that I wanted all nukes to be done away with. One wonders if Sunderji might be sad knowing that tactical nuclear war-fighting, which he considered sinfully escalatory, is now part of current Indian and Pakistani military doctrine . . .

The story of Pakistani nuclear weapons goes back to the defeat of West Pakistan by India in 1971 when East Pakistan, aided by India, separated after a bloody civil war to become Bangladesh. A year later, the Prime Minister of a truncated Pakistan, Zulfiqar Ali Bhutto, called a meeting of Pakistani nuclear scientists in the city of Multan to map out a nuclear weapons programme. Pakistan lacked a strong technological base, but its secret search of the world's industrialized countries for nuclear weapons technologies was successful. After 1979, as the front-line state in the fight in Afghanistan against the Soviets, Pakistan was to feel little pressure from the US. By 1986, with the help of centrifuge technology surreptitiously brought in from Belgium and Holland by Dr AQ Khan, Pakistan had its first atom bomb.

The US response was a series of flips and flops. As a reward for Pakistan's anti-Soviet efforts, US economic and military assistance continued flowing. It was only after the Soviet withdrawal from Afghanistan in 1988 that Washington toughened its stance on Pakistan's nuclear programme.

Then came the Indian nuclear tests of May 1998. Initially reluctant to test, Pakistan was forced over the hill by belligerent statements from Indian leaders. Diffidence soon turned into aggressive triumphalism. Countering India's nukes became secondary. Pakistan would see its weapons as a talisman, able to ward off all dangers.

Breathtaking adventurism followed. Chief of Army Staff General Pervez Musharraf sent non-uniformed troops along with Islamist militant fighters across the Line of Control in Kashmir to seize strategic positions in the high mountains of the Kargil area. Pakistan's nuclear shield would make an Indian response impossible, he reasoned. The subsequent war of 1999 may be recorded by historians as the first actually caused by nuclear weapons.

But, as India counter-attacked and Pakistan stood diplomatically isolated, it agreed to an immediate withdrawal, shedding all earlier pretensions that Pakistan's army had no control over the attackers. Despite this defeat, Pakistan insisted that it had prevailed and that its nuclear weapons had deterred India from crossing the Line of Control or the international border.

Tensions Between Pakistan and India

The comfort of nukes, and a dawning realization that Kashmir could not be liberated by force, was to free the army from its hard life in the trenches. Its attention turned instead towards the pursuit of private wealth. This may explain why Pakistan has the world's richest generals today.

A crisis soon followed. After 11 September 2001, Musharraf's military government insisted there was no danger of any of its nuclear weapons being taking for a ride, but it wasn't taking any chances. The Americans, or some disaffected radical Islamic group, were seen as potential hijackers. Several weapons were airlifted to safer, isolated locations.

Tensions rose in December 2001 after an attack on the Indian parliament by Islamic militants, whom India accused Pakistan of having backed. Nuclear threats started flying in all directions. In May 2002—as fighter aircraft circled Islamabad

Four Scenarios that Threaten Pakistan Nuclear Security

The security of Pakistan's nuclear weapons has been a key concern in recent years with the rise of terrorist and insurgent violence and the expansion of geographical areas under the control of the Taliban in the country. The fear is that such developments increase the likelihood of scenarios in which Pakistan's nuclear security is put at risk; scenarios such as (1) personnel working in Islamabad's [Pakistan's capital] nuclear program collaborate with militant groups and proliferation networks; (2) the Taliban captures nuclear facilities located in western Pakistan as they expand areas under their geographical control; (3) deliberate or inadvertent attacks on Islamabad's nuclear facilities; (4) persistent political instability negatively impacting on the strength of nuclear command and control.

Monterey Institute of Nonproliferation Studies,
"Pakistan: Nuclear Overview," June 2009.

[Pakistan's capital]—in a public debate with me, the former chief of Pakistan's army General Mirza Aslam Beg declared: 'We can make a first strike, and a second strike, or even a third.' The lethality of nuclear war left him unmoved. 'You can die crossing the street,' he observed, 'or you could die in a nuclear war. You've got to die some day anyway.'

Defused by intense Western diplomatic efforts, the crisis eventually faded. Warring with India had begun to look improbable, thanks to the army's 'crown jewels'. Nuclear weapons were seen as anchors of stability, or perhaps magic amulets for warding off the evil eye.

Pakistan's Weapons Might Be at Risk

But today these crown jewels are in danger again—even if the military is unwilling to admit it. Earlier this year [in 2008], as jihadists [those espousing "holy war"] set off bomb blasts aimed at both the military and civilians, the head of the International Atomic Energy Agency, Mohamed ElBaradei said: 'I fear that chaos, or an extremist regime, could take root in that country which has 30 to 40 warheads.' He expressed fear that 'nuclear weapons could fall into the hands of extremist groups in Pakistan or Afghanistan'.

Pakistan's Foreign Ministry swiftly condemned ElBaradei's remarks as 'unwarranted and irresponsible', darkly referring to campaigns orchestrated against Pakistan because 'we are a developing country and we are a Muslim country'. Newspaper editorials and columnists agreed. Pakistan's largest Urdu [national language of Pakistan] daily, *Jang*, accused him of joining the chorus to 'establish Pakistan as an irresponsible state' while *The Nation* said Baradei had 'toed the American line' and compromised his dignity and neutrality. The daily *Ausaf* ran a headline urging the entire nation rally together to save its nuclear weapons. Without them, it argued, Pakistan would forever be at the mercy of India, Israel and America.

The strongest claims for safety come from the Strategic Plans Division (SPD), the part of the Pakistani military tasked with handling nuclear weapons. Its officers are in close contact with Washington, and the SPD was a key beneficiary of a secret $100 million grant to make Pakistan's nuclear weapons safer from the [George W.] Bush administration. Military officers receive training in gadgetry designed to prevent unauthorized use, and to improve storing and custodial procedures, perimeter security and personnel reliability.

The SPD exudes confidence that it can safely protect nuclear weapons, even from Islamic militants. So does Musharraf. Asked by *Newsweek*'s Fareed Zakaria if he thought Pakistan's nukes were safe, Musharaff replied 'Absolutely. [The

SPD] is like an army unit. Can one rifle be taken away from an army unit? I challenge anyone to take a bullet, a weapon, away from an army unit.'

It was a bad challenge to make. Just two weeks later, Taliban militants ambushed a convoy and captured four military trucks on the Indus Highway. Some carried ammunition, while others were transporting military vehicles fitted with sophisticated communications and listening technology. The trucks were recovered a week later—minus their cargo. More significantly, a score of suicide attacks in the past few months, some bearing a clear insider signature, have rocked an increasingly demoralized military and intelligence establishment. An attack on a Pakistan Air Force bus near Sargodha, where nuclear weapons are stored, killed 8 and seriously injured 40. It was masterminded by retired army major, Ahsanul Haq. He was associated with warriors who had fought Pakistan's covert jihad in Afghanistan and Kashmir. Today, some parts of the military and intelligence are at war with other parts.

Pakistan May Be Threatened by Its Weapons

Fearful of more attacks, military officers have limited their wearing of uniforms, move in civilian cars, and no longer flaunt their rank in public. They yearn for the days when the enemy was India, but now they must fight shadows. A senior military officer recently confided in me that he feels especially vulnerable when held up by traffic lights at an intersection. An army in such shape does not inspire confidence in its ability to safeguard nukes.

There are many questions but few answers. Would it be possible for different commanders, each with authorization for different parts of a nuclear weapon? Could jihadist outsiders develop links with sympathetic custodial insiders?

Will radical Islamists acquire the technical expertise, and the highly enriched uranium, needed for a crude nuclear device? Such a weapon could be built secretly.... In Pakistan's weapons laboratories, religious fervour has grown enormously over the past three decades. Given the absence of accurate records of fissile material production, can one be certain that small quantities of highly enriched uranium or weapons-grade plutonium have not already been diverted?

There is little doubt that if extremists succeed in getting nuclear materials, they will not hesitate in using them. One should not assume that London or New York will be the targets; Islamabad and Delhi [India's capital] may be just as good—and certainly much easier. In the twisted logic of the fanatics, there is little or no difference between apostates [one who has abandoned religion] and those who are the tools of apostates. The suicide bombings in mosques and public meetings send exactly this message. As yet there is little realization that Pakistan's nuclear weapons may be even more dangerous to itself than to other countries.

Periodical Bibliography

Missy Adams — "Khan's Dangerous Game," *Time*, February 14, 2005.

M.M. Ali — "Political Stability in Pakistan Increasingly Elusive," *Washington Report on Middle East Affairs*, August 2008.

Rajesh M. Basrur and Sumit Ganguly — "Pakistan's Self-Defeating Army," *Newsweek International*, May 4, 2009.

William F. Buckley Jr. — "Pakistan's Blood-Stained Democracy," *National Review*, January 28, 2008.

Urs Gehriger — "Q&A with A.Q. Khan," *Weekly Standard*, January 27, 2009.

Kenneth M. Luongo and Naeem Salik — "Building Confidence in Pakistan's Nuclear Security," *Arms Control Today*, December 2007.

David Montero — "Violent Debate on Women's Rights in Pakistan," *Christian Science Monitor*, March 6, 2007.

David E. Sanger — "Obama's Worst Pakistan Nightmare," *New York Times Magazine*, January 11, 2009.

James Traub — "Can Pakistan Be Governed?" *New York Times Magazine*, March 31, 2009.

Fareed Zakaria — "This Is Pakistan's War," *Newsweek*, March 3, 2008.

For Further Discussion

Chapter 1

1. After reading the viewpoints in this chapter, what do you think is the most serious problem facing Pakistan? Please support your answer with facts from the viewpoints.

2. In their viewpoints, Sumit Ganguly and *Economic Review* disagree on whether foreign investment has helped or hurt Pakistan's economy. Whose argument do you find more convincing and why?

3. K. Alan Kronstadt argues that madrassas have helped influence anti-American views, while Peter Bergen and Swati Pandey opine that these religious schools are not dangerous. After reading their viewpoints, do you believe that madrassas have a positive or negative affect on Pakistan? Please support your view using the viewpoints and any other relevant readings.

Chapter 2

1. In its viewpoint, Amnesty International argues that Pakistan must not violate human rights in its aim to end terrorism. Do you believe that the fight against terrorism can justify certain human rights violations, in the aim of saving lives? Why or why not?

2. The U.S. Government Accountability Office and Lisa A. Curtis suggest ways in which the United States can reduce the problem of Pakistani terrorism. Whose suggestions do you think would be more effective, and why?

Chapter 3

1. Hassan Abbas is a former member of Pakistan's government. In what ways do you think his background impacts his argument? Please explain your answer.

2. Robert Bryce maintains that the United States lacks leverage over Pakistan because it is too reliant on Pakistani fuel. Do you agree with his assessment? Why or why not?

3. After reading the viewpoints in this chapter, which type of U.S. aid do you believe would be most effective in Pakistan: political, economic, or military? Or, like Charles Scaliger, do you feel that the U.S. should not provide foreign aid to Pakistan? Please explain your answer, drawing from the viewpoints and other relevant material.

Chapter 4

1. Richard N. Haass and William Dalrymple disagree as to whether Pakistan can become politically stable. Whose argument do you find more convincing, and why?

2. Do you agree with Farida Shaheed's argument that the assassination of Benazir Bhutto was a tragedy for the women's movement in Pakistan? Why or why not?

Organizations to Contact

The editors have compiled the following list of organizations concerned with the issues debated in this book. The descriptions are derived from materials provided by the organizations. All have publications or information available for interested readers. The list was compiled on the date of publication of the present volume; the information provided here may change. Be aware that many organizations take several weeks or longer to respond to inquiries, so allow as much time as possible.

Asia Foundation
PO Box 193223, San Francisco, CA   94119-3223
(415) 982-4640 • fax: (415) 392-8863
e-mail: info@asiafound.org
Web site: www.asiafoundation.org

The Asia Foundation is a non-governmental organization that seeks the development of a peaceful and prosperous Asia-Pacific region. It works with private and public partners to help support programs that empower women, improve civil society, and reform these nations' economies. Among the programs it supports in Pakistan are electoral reform, alternative dispute resolution, and women's empowerment. Publications include *Pakistan: Old Problems, New Answers?* and *Government, Health, and Empowerment.*

Center for Strategic and International Studies (CSIS)
1800 K St. NW, Washington, DC   20006
(202) 887-0200
Web site: http://csis.org

CSIS is a bipartisan organization that researches international issues and offers insights and solutions to government, the private sector, and international institutions. Its research focuses primarily on global challenges, defense and security, and regional transformation. Several reports and other publications about Pakistan are available on its Web site, including "The Trilateral Summit: Prospects for U.S., Afghan, and Pakistan Cooperation."

Central Asia Institute (CAI)

PO Box 7209, Bozeman, MT 59771
(406) 585-7841 • fax: (406) 585-5302
e-mail: info@ikat.org
Web site: www.ikat.org

The Central Asia Institute works to improve education in rural areas of Pakistan, Afghanistan, and other parts of Central Asia. It has established 130 schools in Pakistan and Afghanistan, emphasizing the education of girls. Programs supported by CAI include building libraries and training teachers. Articles, videos, publications, and information about the institute's programs are available on the Web site, including "2008 Journey of Hope."

Council on Foreign Relations (CFR)

58 E 68th St., New York, NY 10065
(212) 434-9400 • fax: (212) 434-9800
e-mail: national@cfr.org
Web site: www.cfr.org

The Council on Foreign Relations is an independent, nonpartisan think tank that aims to help people better understand foreign policy issues that are critical to the United States. Its scholars and task force members produce reports and articles that analyze important foreign policy topics. CFR also publishes the journal, *Foreign Affairs*, and an annual report, along with its reports. Articles about Pakistan are available on the Web site.

Heritage Foundation

214 Massachusetts Ave. NE, Washington, DC 20002-4999
(202) 546-4400 • fax: (202) 546-8328

e-mail: info@heritage.org
Web site: www.heritage.org

The Heritage Foundation is a conservative public policy re-search institute that supports limited government, a strong national defense, and traditional American values. The foun-dation believes that the U.S. should support democratic re-forms in South and Southeast Asia. Commentaries, speeches, Congressional testimony, and articles on Pakistan are available on the Web site, including "From Strategy to Implementation: Strengthening U.N.-Pakistan Relations" and "The Pakistan Problem."

Human Rights Watch

350 Fifth Ave., 34th Fl., New York, NY   10118-3299
(212) 290-4700 • fax: (212) 736-1300
e-mail: hrwnyc@hrw.org
Web site: www.hrw.org

The goal of Human Rights Watch is to protect and defend hu-man rights around the world. It investigates human rights violations and seeks to hold abusers, including governments, accountable. Publications about human rights violations in Pakistan include "Destroying Legality: Pakistan's Crackdown on Lawyers and Judges" and "With Friends Like These: Hu-man Rights Violations in Azad Kashmir."

International Center for Religion and Diplomacy (ICRD)

1625 Massachusetts Ave. NW, Suite 601
Washington, DC   20036
(202) 331-9404 • fax: (202) 872-9137
Web site: www.icrd.org

The goal of the ICRD is to use religious reconciliation, along with official or unofficial diplomacy, to help solve identity-based conflicts. By doing so, the center aims to minimize the use of war as a solution. ICRD also works with religious and civic organizations in Pakistan to help the nation's teachers provide their students with a better education. The center's publications include reports and research on Pakistan, such as *Pakistani Madrasas: Questions and Answers.*

Pakistan International Human Rights Organization (PIHRO)

Head Office #12, 1-D, 2nd Fl., Rahmat Plaza
Nazim-ud-Din Rd., Blue Area, PO Box 3040, G.P.O.
Islamabad   Post Code: 44000
   Pakistan
+92-51-2828791 • fax: +92-51-2872092
e-mail: info@pihro.org
Web site: www.pihro.org

PIHRO is an independent non-governmental organization that works to improve human welfare and help those in need. In particular, the organization works with youth throughout Pakistan, as well as Kashmir. Publications include case studies on human rights issues.

United Nations Development Programme— Pakistan (UNDP)

House No. 12, Street No. 17, F 7/2
Islamabad
   Pakistan
Phone: +92-51-8255600 • fax: +92-51-2655014-15
Web site: www.undp.org.pk

UNDP partners with the Pakistani government to help the nation achieve development goals relating to poverty, the environment and energy, democratic governance, and crisis prevention. Projects that the UNDP has worked on with Pakistan include constructing low-cost, energy-efficient homes in certain regions of the nation and developing a program to conserve and improve the environment. Through these and similar efforts, UNDP aims to improve the lives of Pakistan's poor and disadvantaged.

United Nations Industrial Development Organization— Pakistan (UNIDO)

House No. 35, College Rd., Sector F-7/2Z
Islamabad
   Pakistan
e-mail: info@unido.org.pk
Web site: www.unido.org.pk

The mission of UNIDO is to promote sustainable industrial development in developing economies. It helps governments and the private sector work together to develop industrial production, international partnerships, and environmentally friendly industrial practices. It has had an office in Pakistan since 1968, and its efforts in the nation have included the development of engineering institutes.

Bibliography of Books

Hassan Abbas	*Pakistan's Drift into Extremism: Allah, then Army, and America's War on Terror*. Armonk, NY: M.E. Sharpe, 2004.
Tariq Ali	*The Duel: Pakistan on the Flight Path of American Power*. New York: Scribner, 2008.
Craig Baxter, ed.	*Pakistan on the Brink: Politics, Economics, and Society*. Lanham, MD: Lexington Books, 2004.
Brian Cloughley	*War, Coups and Terror: Pakistan's Army in Years of Turmoil*. New York: Skyhorse Publishing, 2009.
Stephen P. Cohen	*The Idea of Pakistan*. Washington, DC: Brookings Institution Press, 2006.
Douglas Frantz and Catherine Collins	*The Man from Pakistan: The True Story of the World's Most Dangerous Nuclear Smuggler*. New York: Twelve, 2008.
Zahid Hussain	*Frontline Pakistan: The Struggle with Militant Islam*. New York: Columbia University Press, 2008.
Adrian Levy	*Deception: Pakistan, the United States, and the Secret Trade in Nuclear Weapons*. New York: Walker and Company, 2007.

Iftikhar H. Malik   *The History of Pakistan*. Westport,
CT: Greenwood Press, 2008.

William B. Milam   *Bangladesh and Pakistan: Flirting with
Failure in South Asia*. New York:
Columbia University Press, 2009.

Greg Mortenson   *Three Cups of Tea: One Man's Mission
to Promote Peace: One School at a
Time*. New York: Penguin Books,
2006.

Shuja Nawaz   *Crossed Swords: Pakistan, Its Army,
and the Wars Within*. New York:
Oxford University Press, 2008.

T.V. Paul   *The India-Pakistan Conflict: An
Enduring Rivalry*. New York:
Cambridge University Press, 2005.

Mohammad   *Pakistan: Social and Cultural
Abdul Qadeer   Transformations in a Muslim Nation*.
London: Routledge, 2006.

Ahmed Rashid   *Descent into Chaos: The U.S. and the
Disaster in Pakistan, Afghanistan, and
Central Asia*. New York: Penguin,
2009.

Saeed Shafqat, ed.   *New Perspectives on Pakistan: Visions
for the Future*. New York: Oxford
University Press, 2007.

James Wynbrandt   *A Brief History of Pakistan*. New
York: Checkmark Books, 2008.

Index